# From Foot Soldier To Elite

# From Foot Soldier To Elite

Lord Priest

authorHOUSE®

*AuthorHouse™*
*1663 Liberty Drive*
*Bloomington, IN 47403*
*www.authorhouse.com*
*Phone: 1-800-839-8640*

*First published by AuthorHouse    07/05/2011*

*ISBN: 978-1-4634-1074-2 (sc)*
*ISBN: 978-1-4634-1401-6 (ebk)*

*Library of Congress Control Number: 2011908846*

*Printed in the United States of America*

## My Dedications

This book is dedicated to the memories of friends,and family whom I've lost along the way to me becoming the author I am today, you may be gone but through my books and stories you will live on and on and never be forgotten.

I would like to give thanks to my mother Rose Ann Waddell and my father Thorton Hudson to my god sisters Suzette Coleman Shijuane Miller to my aunt Rev Ruth Watson and my cousin Clyde Holster to the brothers I came up with in the nation Kenny Doss,Patrick Wisper,Elijah Green,South Side,and my god father Slick ass Rick,to my adopted grandmother Beulah Pittman and my adopted brother Jermaine Allen.

Last but not least I would like to give thanks to my wife Leanya Letcher-Waddell, Jada Davidson, Monica Davidson, Nicole Davidson,Shavonta Williams.And anyone else whom I forgotten.

Where should I start? O yeah from the beginning, I didn't come from a broken home, or a fucked up family on drugs, like most of the people you see in the movies'or on TV. My household was full of love and carring. It was me, my mother, and my father on the Westside of Chicago. Being an only child had its advantages and disadvantages. I always had lots of toys to play with, because my mom was a nurse and my dad a Cook County Sheriff; I was spoiled to the tee. Since I didn't have a brother or a sister to play with, coming up my mother and father would take me to my cousins' house to play with them. I had a cousin named Mandell who was one or two years older then me. He had a big sister named Melissa and a little brother named Stacey. I would love going over their house, because it was lots of fun playing with someone close to my age. It was one of the best times of my life, until when I was about nine, when the lady who I had thought was my aunt took me in her room and told me something that would change my whole life. She said, "I'm not your aunt, I'm your grandmother". I replied, "No you're not, you're my mother's sister". "No I'm your grandmother." she said In. amazement I asked, "what do u mean?" she answered and said, she's your great-aunt' who you call your mother, Rose". Is, my sister "Rose is not my mother?" she nodded then said, "No Jean, is Mandell's mother is also your mother". Lost in thought I said, "So Mandell is not my cousin, he's my brother and Melissa is my sister, Stacey my brother?" "Yes they are". Confused I asked, "So why don't I live with you?" She told me I would have to ask my mother, so I left the back room of the house, and went into the front room. I knocked on Jean's door and asked to come in. I went in and close the door and told jean I had something to ask.her with a confused look, she asked, "what?" With no hesitation, I asked, "Are you my mother?" "Who told you that?" was her response. "My grandmother", I said boldly. "Who's your grandmother, Aunt Mildred? Mildred comes here! Why did you tell this boy that?"Mildred yelled. "Because you won't and I think its time that he know jean; jean yelled back. "You make me sick! Get out of my room!" "No you make me sick! I'm your mother, you're not mine, I'll leave your room, not because you said get out but because I think you need to talk to him." Talk to your mother boy." She then left and closed the door behind her. Jean said nastily, "what do you want now!" I replied, "Why don't I live with you?" I don't know what she said after that, but I couldn't understand, I guess I was too young but I asked her could I stay with her. She told me yes and I was so happy. I ran to tell Mandell. When I reached him I said, "Guess what, I'm not your cousin, I'm your brother!" With a shocked look on his face he said, "For real!" "Yes and jean said I can stay!" we were so happy and we played all day. My great aunt came back to give me some money, so I told her I knew she was my great aunt and that it was cool. It was the weekend and I thought I was going to stay forever, but Sunday came and so did she. She had came to get me and take me home, but I ran into Jean's room and started shouting, "You said I could stay, you said I could stay". She looks at me and said, "Boy, you got to go to school, you'll be back on the weekend". My response was, "I can go to school from here!" she yelled, "Boy get your butt out of here". I screamed, "You're not my mother, you're not my mother!" I cried hard until I went to sleep. When I got up I was at home. Rose had taken me in the house and sat me down to talk to me. But before she got her first word out I yelled, "You don't love me." she replied, "Yes I do love you!" I said, "But I don't have any other kids to play with over here, the Southside kids don't like me because I'm a Westside kid, I can't even go outside and play." She answered with tears in her eyes, "Don't you think about them, you have your own toys and you don't have to play with them if you don't want to. I'm still your mother, now go to sleep and I'll talk to you in the morning.

The next few years went by fast and it didn't matter that my mother was my great aunt and my father was my great uncle. They gave me lots of love and everything a kid could want. I loved them just the same. It was close to my 12th birthday and my father use to take me to the drive-inn on the weekends. There he would teach me how to drive before the movie started. On my 12th birthday he bought me a car. I was only in 6th grade and was driving to school! The teachers use to look at me like I was crazy or something, but it was cool. School had just started after summer break, and I had a new teacher, her name was Ms. Towner. She was a good looking black woman, who took no shit. Her and my mother became good friends because my mothers use to bring me lunch everyday to school. Ms. Towner had seen that my mother had retired from being a nurse. She had opened a candy store and it had video games in it and all the candy in the world! Every kid in the hood knew me, I was 12 years old driving my own car, and my mother owned the best candy store around, I had went from having no friends at age 9 to having the whole hood being my friends at age 12. My close friends were older then me, like the twins Larry and Terry, then there was Tony, and big Tyrone, Billy, and Stanley. But I mostly hung out with the twins, Larry and Terry. We did everything together. We went to the movies; we went skating, normal kid stuff. They put me up on how to dress. It was the late 70's and everybody was wearing tailor maids and Stacey Adams and had finger waves or butters as we use to call them. It was a great time in my life. Larry, Terry, and I use to go to Skate City on the weekend to dance and step. They were real good and they taught me how to step. Going to Skate City was my first lesson about gang banging. We were at Skate City one night, and this guy named Rubin was talking crazy to Terry about something that happened at school. I wasn't there being that they were in high school and I was only in 6th grade. He came over to where I and Terry were standing and started talking crazy. "Now talk that shit you were talking in school", was the first thing he said when he walked up. Terry told him to get the fuck out of his face before he beat his ass. Rubin just looked and walked away. I thought it was over, because we all started skating again. It was almost time for the skating to end, and the dancing to begin. Terry and I put our skates up and our shoes on and went to the party. Everything seemed cool, Larry and everybody else who had came with us, were out on the dance floor, when rubin and two other guys walked up to us and Rubin said, "These are the niggas I was talking about". Not knowing what was going on, Larry said, "What the fuck are you talking about Rubin?" Rubin thought Larry was Terry, but then Terry walked up and Rubin was looking stupid. The other two guys never said one word. Then one of the guys put on a black glove and put his fist in the air. It looked like the whole Skate City was around us, then one of the guys said, "What up you hooks coming in here, Like we won't beat ya'll ass out here" Larry responded saying, "Who's a hook? I am not a hook, I'm Folks." The guy looked at Rubin confused and said, "I thought you said they were hooks". "Man I don't know if he's a hook, but his brother is." rubin replied. Terry said, "Nigga you know me and my brother is Folks, you just mad because I took your girl, and you're just too much of a mark ass buster to fight Me." rubin responded saying, "Man fuck that bitch if I wanted her back, and I could get her with no problem." The guy finished Rubin's sentence, "anyway we don't fight Folks over any bitch as nigga, you on some bullshit." At that time

Bobby came over and said, "What the fuck is going on over here Mike Hikkie, I know you and Pickels ain't over here trying to beat up on my little brother?" "Man Bobby Reed these are your little brothers. We didn't know you're Bobby's little brothers, we know you got to be Folks. Rubin we should beat your ass for lying to us. He told us your little brothers were some Hookes Bobby." looked at Rubin and said, "What this lil nigga right here?" He lifted his hand and smacked the hell out of Rubin. Then said, "He is in-v he is in-v get him" when he said that they beat his ass to the ground, and then threw his ass out of Skate City and went back to parting. The guys that were with him came up to shake our hands and told us their names, Mike Hikkie and Pickels, then went to get us some pops. We partied until it was time to go. On the way out I went up to Bobby Reed to introduce myself. When I started to he stopped me and said, "Boy I know you, you're Rose's son, the candy store lady, me, your mother and your father are good friends." When he noticed the party was over he told us to take our ass's home and not to get into any bullshit. I called my mother to come pick us up and asked her did she know Bobby, she said, "Yes, Bobby is your friends, Terry and Larry, big brother. He lives down the street with them. Remember when them boys took you're bike from you? He was the one that got it back for me, he's good people. I know all the Reeds." she ended the call by saying she was on her way. After she hung up it didn't take long for her to get there. We lived on 56th and Skate City was on 63rd. When we got home I told her what had happened, she told me Bobby was a B.G.D.N. I asked her what that meant, she told me Black Gangster Disciples. I wanted to know more, so I asked more questions like what's a Black Gangster Disciples. She told me it was a gang so I asked what a gang was. She said it was a group of people who run the hood. Full of interest I shouted, "I want to be a B.G.D.N." She turned around so fast and she looked at me with the most serious face I had ever seen from her and said, "No you're not going to be in anybody's gang, you hear me boy." I said ok and went in to my room. I wasn't sleepy, so I called Terry and Larry house. Terry answered the phone with a greeting of who is this? I told him it was me and asked him was he sleepy, he said no so we talked for a while. I started by saying "Hey are you a B.G.D.N". His answer was, "No, but all my big brothers are and Larry too. But Larry just got into it, we should get in". I asked how would we get in. he said by going to one of the meetings, which were held behind the school on Sundays. So we had decided that we would go to the next meeting next Sunday. That shit I had seen in skate city was the coolest shit I had ever seen in my life, and I couldn't wait until Sunday came to go to the meeting. I was in school asking people did they know about the B.G.D.N. some people knew and some just looked at me like I was crazy, and responded, who doesn't know about the B.G.D.N. As it got closer to the weekend, terry and I couldn't stop talking about the meeting. We had a lot of questions, like what we were suppose to do when we got there, or what we were suppose to say, so terry asked his brother Larry. What do they do at the meetings larry asked, why do you want to know he told him.because we were going to go to the meeting this Sunday he said ok just when you get there just be cool.when they open the meeting just let them know you want to become a new member of the nation, and they will let you know what you have to do to become new members. So larry asked terry why do you want to be a BGDN because everybody is but me ok.im going to be there so let me talk for you and I can get you in.but how about you get the both of us in I don't know he looks kind of young ,and we don't have much to say about him.but one of the first Cs can get him in just be on time the meeting starts at 4:00 pm on Sunday just be on time.its Friday night we where at the Friday night skate city rink.doing what we do skating and getting with the females and stepping,but that night was like no other night we had just got a nigga a v—and people knew us as bobby reed lil brothers and homies.we became real cool with mike hikkie and pickles.so after that night everybody knew us.it was so cool to know pickles he had all the females and being with him was the shit.so that's why me and terry hung around. Pickles had one main lady name pam she was cool with all the other females.she looked so fine and had a body out of this world.she could skate her ass off, and step really good to.she was one of the coldest females I had ever seen in my life.to be 13 years old pam and pickles were the shit.so me and terry hung around. Pam would always have a lot of females hanging around and she would hook us up with some of the best looking girls in skate city. Me and terry were in the pool room withs some girls and pickles came in and said hey yall come with me its some niggas in here fucking with pam.so me and terry was ready to beat some niggas ass for fucking with pam and pickles.so we walked over to the food court with pickles were pam was and he said pam weres that nigga she pointed and said there he is.pickles walked over and said whats up with you fucking with my girl and me and terry just started stealing off his ass. And before you knew it half of skate city was beating his ass the poolroom the skating floor all of that is in skate city.after that pickles would come down were we were hanging and kick it with us because he knew we had his back.and plus pam hooked us up with some of the finest girls around.she had hooked terry up with this fine ass girl name tammie and I was always there to get the hook up with the li brother lil sister hook up thang,but I always had me a fine ass chick to go to the movies with when I walked up in skate city but it wasn't about that we were still thinking about the meeting now its Sunday moring and me and terry couldn't wait until 4:00.we went bought new clothes so everybody would recongize us.we shoped up on 63$^{rd}$ street.when we got back it was about 3:30.we got dressed walked up to the Bontemps we got their about 3:45.its already 60 to70 peoples there Im like damm its alots of niggas here some we knew already from the block some from skate city some we never seen before it was like a trip then some of the old Gs came in they were wearing their 6 point stars with their black and blue and you knew they meant no bull shit.they made us get in and gather around each other and said the BGDN law.it sounded like poetry to me.we were told to say our names and where we were from and who told us about the meeting.when it was me and terrys turn larry and bobby spoke for us.larry said me and my brother would like the nation to admit these two new brothers in to the brother hood of black gangster disiples.how bringes these two brothers it's me larry foot soliders of the bgdn. And me bobby,first cs of 56 to 63 street bring them up for membership.so another man said does anybody have cause that these brother not have membership.now okay you two need your dues of 20.00 next meeting ok.the meeting was over and when we got outside they pulled me to the side and said you know you to young to be with us ,but we have meetings for the lil brothers and you can attend those there on Saturdays at 3:30 so next Saturday come up here I said okay and me and terry went home. Terry was happy in all but he was worried about the 20.00 dues. So I told him I would give it to him out of my allowance on next Saturday. Saturday came and terry came to my house he knocked on the door and I opened it he said are you going to give me the money. I said here you go, I had to be at the meeting at 3.30 and he had to be at the meeting at 4.00 clock I said I'm on my way he said I'll see you later I got to the meeting and it was a lot of cats my age some from my school some from the block but no skate city cats just me.the meeting started and they asked who all had their dues some had 5 dollars some had 7 and 10 I'm the only one had my whole 20.the older gs said this lil nigga ain't playing he want to be down for real.I said yes I do want to be down and I asked whats the money for. He said I'm glad you asked he said nobody never asked.he said after the meeting we buy weed and drinks and food.so for asking the question nobody never asked you get the spot over all the pee wee disciples.I see you got sense.I was real happy like had just become the king of the world.so he gave me a paper with everybodys name and phone number on it.it was my job to call everybody and let them know not to miss the meeting if the meeting were at another place.I had been doing this for almost a year I was about to be 14.it was time for me to be a young disciples and stop being a pee wee disciples. Then something happened that I though would never happen.my father got real real sick. it changed my whole life.he went to the hosiptal and stayed a long time.I stop going to meeting and the brothers understood.some would come over and see how I was doing they knew how much I loved my father.a couple of them knew my father.it was the worst time of my life watching my dad die and their was nothing I could do.my mom started getting sick worrying about my dad.I tried to keep her mind off of it.but she just couldn't take it.they had been together for 25 years.that's a long time for a person to be with somebody.me and my mom would go over to Englewood hospital sometimes twice a day.we would get to his room and he would look up and smile.he started to get better and then he came back home for a little while.then righ back he went.then he was sent to the cook county hosiptal.I just knew he was going to get better but he got worst.then one day my mom told me that she had to send me away for a while.then a dcfs worker came and picked me up.I looked and told my mom not to worry about my dad.she told me she would come and see me when she felt better and you can come back home.but my mom knew better.I said okay then I left with the lady. she took me to a group home it was full of kids just like me who's mom and dad was sick.my caseworker was named miss Johnson.she told me that I wouldn't be in the group home long my mother would be back to get me as soon as she felt better.it would be about 3 weeks at the most Herrick house in barrlette Illinois.I had never been that far from home before so I was kind of nervous.the ride to the home was a long ride it took a long time to get there.but when I got there it was big like a mansion it looked like something on tv that every kid wished to live in.when I went in all the kids were sleep so they let me take a shower and get ready for bed.the next morning when I got up' I got washed up.and was taken to the main dining room for breakfast it was a big room.it had about 30 chairs to a table.the girls came in from the other side of the mansion ,and it was a lot of good lookings girls in the bunch.but I was looking at the food at the time I was hungry.it was so much of food we could eat forever.I sat next to a guy named john he had been there for at least two years.his mom and dad died in a car accident,and he had no other family members.he told me how the Herrick house was ran.another case worker came to me to talk she called me by name and took me to another room.it was her office she said have a sit. She began to ask lots of questions like do you know where you are, do you know why you here. I said yes my mom told me as soon as her and dad was feeling better she was going to come and get me. so she ask me what I liked to do,and I said dancing and skating,stepping.she said boy you don't know any thing about stepping.I told her ive been stepping since I was twelve.she said okay we do things like that around here too.she said would you like to call your mom,I said yes,she dialed and handed me the phone my mom answered.I said hey mom she said hey boy do you like it there I"ll be to see you soon and bring you some more clothes some music and some money.okay ill be there this weekend so let me talk to your caseworker.I handed the phone to her.I heard her say he's alright.she looked at me and said you can go back now,so I went back to my side of the building when I got there was no one there.where's everybody staff said at school I asked when was I going to school,he said in two or three days.so I went and sat in the tv room and watched tv until everybody got out of school.when school was out I asked john do we get do anything besides sit here all day.he said no we get to do what ever we want.after dinner he took me to show me the other parts of the mansion on the other side was roomes with games and a tv room were we can watch tv with the girls.a very large backyard.in the back of the yard was a lake. John was my new best friend. he told me about his girl her name was lilbit she was on the south side of the mansion.and we were on the north.john liked basketball and talked me into playing.we played all the time it was fun.everything at the Herrick house was cool.I started to get the hang of things the program was a good one ,we worked on things that was needed.my mom came and brought me some clothes she then left.so I went to put my things away I liked the Herrick house it was nice.couple of days later I got a phone call from my mom she told me that she was coming to get me and it wasn't going to be for long.she got there and she took me to the hospital to see my dad.when we got to his room he looked at me and smiled.little did I know that this would be my last time seeing him.alive he looked at me and told my mom to leave the room after she left he took me by the hand he had a look like he didn't know how to explain what he wanted to say he told me to sit down and he said you know I love you and I don't have much time left.but I want you to look for your brother,I said who mandell,stace no he said you have another brother he older than mandell and his name is curtis he lives on the Westside around homan and monoroe.I wish I could take you to see him myself.I asked when you get out can you take me. he just look and smiled tell your mom to come back in.he talked to her for awhile and then we left.she asked me did I want any thing before I take you back to the group home.I looked and said yes some more music.okay we started for the record store and got some more music and some food I wasn't to go back until the next day.so when we got to the house I called larry and terry to come over.larry was out west at his mom and terry came over to see me.so terry was asking me how the group home was and when are you coming home for good.I said I don't know but I can come on the weekends. so come next weekend so we can go to skate city.I asked him was he still going to the meeting,he told me off and on.he said it anit been the same since you been gone.we were suppose to be in it together.he said fuck does niggas it was cool when you were with me.so I told him I got to get up in the morning to go back to the group home.I'll call you before I go back.I went in and got ready for bed and went to sleep got up the next morning mom made a big breakfast we ate and I packed up and we left.we got to the group home I kissed her and said goodbye. soon as I got in john ran up to me and said man I couldn't hardly wait until you got back.guess who been looking for you.who he said guess I said man I don't have time for this.who ,lisa man she thought you was gone for good she started tripping she had said she was going to make you her boyfriend. I told him don't be bullshiting me. So the next day when we went to breakfast we sat down at a table lilbit and lisa sat across from us lilbit said my girl likes you.lisa hit lilbit girl I can talk for myself.so lisa looked at me and said do you have a girlfriend.I looked at her and said do you have a boyfriend.she said no.so would you be my boyfriend or what I don't look good to you. I said yes so would you be my boyfriend,yes well we'll get together after school.so me and john went back to our side of the building.john said I told you I told you man.she looks good man.I know man you're a happy motherfucker.hell yeah.all that day I couldn't wait for school to get out.so when school was out we had to

Go back to our side of the building.I put on my best outfit and hooked up my hair.we went to the game room and I brought some of my records and soon as lisa saw me she walked over to me and gave me a kiss and boy did I feel like I was on top of the world.I put on a record and started to dance me and lisa john and lilbit were dancing and we were having a good time.it was like nobody was in the room but us.I've had so much fun that night that I was glad to be back.we kicked it until it was time for bed.when it was time for us to go back to our side of the building lisa gave me a big kiss and hug and said goodnite.at that point I knew she really liked me.me and john was walking back and he got this saying like butter baby and gave me a high five.we got back to our side of the building he went to his side of the building he was he was on the west wing and me on the north wing.so when I got in my room I talked to one of the guys to move to the Westside of the building so john could move to my room.he got moved and we kicked it sometimes all night.it was getting close to the weekend and we were going skating so I called my mom and told her not to pick me up.I asked her to tell terry that I was not coming she said ok you really like it there,yes and I told her about lisa.she said will you be coming home next weekend I told her yes. I love you mommy and we said goodbye. the next morning we had to do our chores we got up real early so we could get it out the way.we had to do the bathroom and tv room.we got down on it and did it real good.when we were through we went to the back of the yard to smoke. because it was a no smoking building.while we were smoking and talking I asked john were can we go to be with the girls alone.he said when we go skating we went to the skating rink but it was nothing like skate city all the music was not like the music that we listen to.they didn't even skate like us,but it was cool because lisa was there.we were having fun ,but before we knew it ,it was time to go back to the group home.when we got back it was time to go to bed.lisa gave me a kiss and said goodnite.we went to our room and talked until we fell asleep.the next morning we were talking me and john I was telling him about skate city and he said he wished he can come.we got ready and went to breakfast.he told me today is your lucky day,I said what do you mean. he said I told you I was going to take you to my spot,all yeah I said to myself,I said were is it he said be cool wait until to night boy.I know you are going to tear lisa's ass up.I looked at him and said I'm going to be able to get me some pussy there.hell yeah that's why it's my spot.I looked at john and said man I love you.john said we'll go when no one is looking they will think were in the game room.it was time for dinner we were getting washed up and john handed me a condom.I looked at him and said whats this for he answered and said so you don't get her knocked up.he told me to put it on my dick and do my thang.we got in the dinner hall and lisa was there so I asked her was she up with it and she said yes.boy I couldn't wait until dinner was over.one of the case worker came over to me and said it the phone for you she took me to her office and I picked up the phone and hear my mom crying I said mom what's wrong.she said its your dad he died.at that moment I froze I only knew one person to die and that was a girl that went to school with me she had a seizure and died in the bath tub that was the first funeral I had ever been too. Now my dad had died.I was very shaken by the news I took it real hard when I came out the office.I was still crying when I got back to the table lisa asked me what was wrong I told her my dad had died.she hugged me and gave me a kiss on the forehead.john came over and asked what was going on and lisa told him that my dad had just died. they took me outside but as we were leaving the staff asked was I going to be alright.I answered and said yes.we were standing out front and john said I know you feel bad.but come with me were going to see if we can make you feel better.he took us to the back of the mansion and he come out of his pocket with some weed.we got high then he took us to a part of the building that was closed down it had beds in it.we went in and he asked me if I had that condom.I said yes he said okay handle your business so me and lisa went in and had sex it was the best sex I had ever had.it took my mind off my dad for a while.when we were through we waited on john and lilbit to get through.when we got back in the nick of time it was time for us to go to bed.lisa told me she'll see me in the morning.when I got in bed I began to think and at this point I knew I would never be the same.I feel asleep but when I got up the next morning it felt like I hadn't slept at all.but I got on up and got ready for breakfast and every body tried to make me feel better.I was there but my mind was some were else.my mind just stayed on my dad and what he told me about my other brother.my dad always told me that I was a Westside kid' and told me about the people that I hung around wasn't good for me,he said when you get older you will know what I'm talking about he told me I'm not a southsider their a different in the Westside and the southside and your not a southside kid.I could remember him talking about the boys that I would meet with on Sundays I'm looking at him like how he knows about that things that he said to me just stayed in my head I couldn't get out of my mind.one of the staff came in and told me it was the phone andwhen I got to the phone it was my mom she said she was coming to get me and I was going to stay with her for aboutd a week I hung up and went to pack some clothes so I got done packing and told my friends that I would be gone for about a week to prepare for my dad's funeral.lisa said make sure you come back because I love you and I want to be with you.I told her that I would be back and don't you get another boyfriend.she said I want she said boy don't play with me.if it had not been for lisa I don't know what I might have done.I would have went crazy but her smile seen me through. I didn't know what love was but I guess that's what I was feeling at 14 could

I be in love we spent allday together walking all around the inside and outside of the building.we went to our spot and made love two or three times I spent all day with her because I knew the next morning I would be leaving.she said she wished she could come so I called up my mom and asked she said she didn't care but the Herrick house said no.the next morning I got up about 9:00 but breakfast wasn't until 10:00.lisa was already up waiting on me.I walked out and seen her and started to smile I was hoping my mom had got there before breakfast.while I was thinking it my mom came in.I was so happy to see her. I said mom this is lisa this is the girl I was talking about and lisa said please to meet you.I could see in mom eyes that she was happy not for herself but for me.but I could also see she was heart broken over the death of my father.they had been together for 25 years.and true love like that is hard to fine.they had a love for each other that was going to be hard to live without each other.so I knew I was going to have to look out for her.we started out for our house.on the way home we talk about my dad and things he use to say and do.and before we knew it we were at home. everybody was looking at us when we got to our building.I cant describe the look but it was like it was everybody father.everybody came and gave us a hug.and ask was their anything they could do for us.I took my things to my room and when I got their my room just didn't look the same but all the same stuff was their.but it just looked strange to me.I guess I was so use to being by my self that the was one of the reasons that it felt strange ,but I had got use to living with lots of people and them being around all the time and that what I was getting use too.I turned on my tv and started watching tv.I finally got use to it after 2 days and started calling terry.but he was at his mom house out west. but he would be back in time for my dad's funeral.the funeral arrangment was made for next week. we had family from out of town that needed to get here.grandmom have made it to our house to help mom do what needs to do for funeral arrangments.it was getting close to the weekend and I was thinking about skate city so I could let my hair down and keep my mind off my dad.I had something to look forward to because I enjoyed being at skate city.all week I sat and watched tv and looking at pictures of my dad.thinking how was life going to be without him he was my pride and joy.I knew it was going to be a long time before I really got over his death and accepted it.I had to get to the point of accepting it for my mom that's what he would wanted me to do.so now it's the weekend and I'm getting myself ready for skate city and my cousin bobby comes from upstairs her and her mother june lived upstairs with their family.her mother june had 3 children.her kids bobby and dewayne were older than me.clyde was younger than me.my dad use to take us to the drive-in movies. kids from the hood too.my cousin bobby came down stairs and said come on cuz with me I didn't know what bobby had planned for the night.when june had left bobby came in with some weed and said here you need this more than me.she rolled up a few joints and we started smoking.she started talking about my dad saying uncle dick this,uncle dick that.we sat and smoked until my mom called upstairs and asked was I going to skate city.I answered yes so I asked bobby did she want to go she said no I'll stay here.call me when you get back and we can smoke these other joints,alright then I went down stairs to my house and waited for my mom to drop me off at the rink.she came in the dinning room and asked me if I wanted to drive myself.I said cool and she gave me the keys.she knew that I could drive because my dad taught me.I runs upstairs and tell my cousin bobby to come with me.I had the keys to drive and I didn't want to be alone in the car alone.she said ok grabs her things and we left. we kicked it. I liked hanging around with bobby.she was one of the coolest females I knew.she was pretty and sexy.if she wasn't my cousin I'll be all over her,like all the niggas in the hood was.when we got to skate city everybody was looking like their to young to be driving I was only14 and bobby 16 and we were by ourselves.everybody saying they must got money.me and bobby went alone with it to the tee.we went inside and all the girls was all over me.some of them even thought bobby was my girl.me and my cousin was just having a good time.I looked and saw pam. I asked pam what's up.she looked up at me like I was crazy and then remembered who I was ,and said whats up.were you been long time no see.I've been living out of town,and my dad died and I'm here for the funeral.im sorry to hear that she said.where's the twin and your crew she says their on the Westside at their moms.I asked about pickles and mike hickey.around here some were.she asked who are you up here with I told her that I was with my cousin she's around here some were.you know I don't mess with pickles no more.what happend,see he wanted to be with every girl he could. Be with up in skate city.and I'm suppose to be the dumb bitch that don't know no better,so I let his ass go.but that don't mean were not still cool.okay and I'll see you later.then I walked off.hey pickles what's up nigga.man where in the hell you been ive seen the twins but not you.I've been out of town.are you back now.no my father died and I'm here for the funeral.I'm sorry to hear that so are you okay.I'm alright ,are the twins up here with you no I'm up here with my cousin. what he look like.he's not a he it's a she,well what she look like.she lookes good.we'll let me meet her.you know I don't mess with pam no more.so I listen to his side of the story and we got on the skate floor.we had a good time.its about time to leave I goes and get in the car pam walks over to the car and say who's car.it's my moms bobby comes and get in.this must be your cousin.pam this is bobby bobby pam what's up.pickles spot us and comes over dude I didn't know you had your own car.it's my moms.man drop me off at home he gets in then pam ask if I can take her home I said cool.we left and started on our way. Bobby asks pickle do he smoke weed.yeah she passes him a joint to light up.pickles ask what time we had to be home.we got a little time.well lets go to the park.we got to the park and finished smoking the joints that bobby brought,then she was ready to go,by now she digging pickles and ask me to get out the car I warned her that pam is pickles x.but she didn't care she still wanted to hook up with him.we all gets back in the car and go to the store and I tell pickle to go in with me.we needed some top papers pickles knew the people in the store so we were able to get two six packs.we were to young to buy it while walking back to the car I tell him that bobby likes him.let her get in the back with me.what about pam what about her she's not my girl no more.I think she likes you anyway so let her get up front with you.hey pam get up front with me with a wink.we get to the park and chill some more.smoking and drinking pam's smiling real hard I said what's wrong she says let's get out the car she began with I think your hot.yeah pam was tripping me out telling me how she always had a thing for me and she always wanted to tell me but she was kicking it with pickles,and that wouldn't been cool.so I kept it to myself.man pam looked so good but I couldn't stop thinking about my dad.so I asked pam what she would do if her dad had passed.I don't know might have went crazy.I think I just might be going crazy.I told her all about my dad and how he use to be,.the good times we've had.she looked at me and said don't you start that crying out here.your father is in a better place now.that what everybody been telling me.but I don't see it that way,so let talk about something else.like you really digging me and not telling me.all of pickles friends was trying to get with me.but you and the twins were really his friends and didn't come at me.that's why I liked you.you mean to tell me that mike hickey too. yeah he was the one who tried the most.get out of here so what made you like me.every time I seen you. you were looking good and acted like you had some sense.me and my girls always use to sit and talk about you and how fine you was.you know that's why I use to hook you up with girls because I couldn't have you. I don't want to make pickles mad.man that nigga had his chance and blew it so what's up with you nigga.don't tell me you don't have a girl friend.yeah her name is lisa she lives in the same town that I do.don't tell me that you don't have a girl in Chicago.no,don't lie to me. im not lying.so anyway I think you are a nice guy and I might give you a chance if you play your cards right. so what do you think pickles going to say.who cares look at him.we looked in the car and him and bobby was kissing.I knocked on the window and said get a room then laughed.dont let them,have all the fun. then she grabbed me and started kissing me out of the blue.pam was a sexy thang I almost pissed on myself.her ass was so soft and her lips blew my mind.almost made me forget about my daddy.all I could think about was I cant believe this is happening to me.we were making out in the park me and pam.time sure flys when your having fun.we exchanged number and I dropped them off.so when we got to pam's house pickles got out to so I said do you both live in the same house and she says he lives upstairs.that's how we started kicking it.bobby get your ass in this front seat so we can go.on the way home I asked bobby did she think they were fucking around.she said if we weren't cousin we'll be in the back seat fucking,and we laughed.and we went in the house and I called pam and they said she was sleep,bobby called pickles and was told the same thing.everybody was sleep so we went back to the car and finished our joints then went in the house and went to sleep.the next day bobby came and got me and we went upstairs and I knew she always had weed.we roll up and starts to smoke and the bell rings.it's linda,bobby girl from the block.she was black as tar.but had the biggest titts I have ever seen at my age of 14 years old.she talked a lots of shit so. I would talk crazy to her every chance I got.I said hey linda when you gonna let me suck your tittie.boy you suck these tittie it want be rose's store it'll be linda's store.let me suck one of those big titt and you can have the store.man leave her alone.by the way sorry to hear about your dad. Now im thinking about my daddy again.bobby tells linda why you say something about his dad that's why he's up here with me.light up the weed and stop tripping.and give him some.what some pussy.no stupid the weed.bobby you crazy no you crazy.linda passed the weed and told me that tony been asking about me.I told here to tell him whats up.that's my boy from the hood linda's brother.bobby comes in telling linda about what happened last night.all yall went out and didn't come and get me.girl my aunt roe gave him the car,and we just went skating had a ball girl.you should have stop and got me what happened.I met this nigga name pickles we kicked it and went to the park and smoke kind a digging that nigga too. just the two of you went.no all of us.this nigga had his x with us in the car.girl for real.yeah we were getting down like grown people girl.we had weed two six packs.did you fuck him.,no he didn't have a condom,you should've let him put it in and when he was cumming he could've took it out.hell no I don't get down like that with some nigga I don't even know.what was that mark doing.he was getting down with the nigga'es x. this mark almost got him some pussy. not this mark in the park yeah girl.yeah I could've suck does big titts too.don't start that shit boy.bobby got mad and sent me down stairs.but I didn't care I was already high.went in the house into my room the phone rings and its pam.what you doing.nothing just got through getting high with my cousin and she put me out. can I come over.yeah if you want to.be there in a few the other line click it's lisa hold on lisa yeah pam I told pam where I lived.okay ill be there.hung up from pam and click over.hey baby what's up what you been doing miss me.you know I do what you doing.just got high with my cousin and she kicked me out.tell her don't do that or im come and kick her butt.no we play like that.so what's been up with you.nothing wishing you were here with me.last night we went skating last night and had a good time got a chance not to think about my dad.don't you wish I was there to go with you.yeah it popped in my head.I wasn't even thinking of her because pam had me tied up and blew my mind.so I asked her what every body was doing.every body is okay.tell them I said hello I'll see them when I get back.tell john to hold it down until I get back.okay my phone time is up I'll talk to you later.mom came to the door it's a girl at the door for you.mom let pam in and showed her to my room she came and sat on the bed.you have anything to drink.I goes in the kitchen and get her a pop.she was checking my room out.nice room you have.thanks it's cool,she lean over and gave me a kiss and asked did I have some weed.no but my cousin do.we then goes and ring the doorbell the minute she comes to the door she starts to talk shit until she see pam then she say whats up girl and lets us in.she tell me don't get up here and start acting like you did before and make me put your ass out again.you know I'm not on that cuz you got some weed.no you got some money.I got up and went down stairs mom you got some money she handed me 20 dollars and said that's coming out of your allowance,ok don't stay out late im right upstairs with bobby and pam.she ask me what you need money for,were playing cards.when I got back upstairs I said were's your money we put our money together and bought some weed,we got high and set around talking.I pulled bobby to the side and said I want to get me some pussy. the condoms are in my drawer,what time is june going to be coming home.about one in the morning.I thought good.her and linda left,I went back to the room pam says how long is your cousin going to be why she lean over and we started kissing she put her hands in my pants and mine in hers I took her pants down.here comes bobby and linda back in the room.linda starts to laugh we thought we were going to see some thing I knew he was a mark.I bet he didn't even try and get a kiss.mark.I thought to my self with her black big tittie ass.pam says what you thought when we heard you coming he was going to put his dick in.I pulled bobby in the next room and said whats up with that you need some time cuz wear a condom don't let that bitch set your dick on fire.there in the top drawer.we are going to roll the weed up in kitchen cuz don't be long we are trying to get high.I went back in the room with pam and went right to work,started kissing she said nigga get out of does pants,I thought to myself I never took my pants all the way off,but what the hell she had hers off.she takes her shirt off and wow some nice ass titties not to big and not to little.so I went right to sucking them.I started kissing her neck and just as I was going to stick my dick in I thought about what bobby had said about the condom and I grabed one and put it on.right in the pussy I went,the pussy was so good I thought I was in pussy heaven.fucking her was like nothing I had ever had I almost had forgot that it was not my first time we did our thang.we got done and put our clothes on and went in the kitchen with bobby and linda and started to get high.linda looked at me and said you finally got you some pussy and she laughed.maybe you want be a mark now.I started to say something but I just kept my cool.bobby was looking at me and laughing she passed the joint and beer.and said cuz you the man today.linda kept looking at me but wouldn't say shit it was tripping me out.pam smoked two joints and was ready to go.linda's big mouth ass gonna say something now all you want to do is go get some real dick now.pam looked at her and said that was some real dick I just got need to get you some. she said you'll take me home I said let me ask my mom for the car,I goes down stairs and say mom can I use the car to take pam home were do she live.right by skate city. come right back.goes up stairs to get pam asks bobby do she want to ride I knew linda's big mouth ass had to ride.didn't even trip because she's bobby's girl.we get in and take pam home and soon as we pull up to pam's building we see pickles ass.he's looking at us like we crazy,why you didn't call.I did they told me you were sleep.why you didn't call the next day.I'll call you when I get home.we pulled off.bobby starts talking I anit calling that nigga I believe that nigga fuck pam's ass that night.I'm thinking I don't care because she got some good ass pussy.linda askes bobby who she was talking about. she said the bitch that cuz just fucked.what that use to be his hoe yeah then she started fucking him who bryon yeah.when we got back linda's brother tony was in front of the building mommy want you.linda left.I took my mother her keys and went back upstairs and started to get high some more.hey bobby you think I should make pam my girlfriend.hell no because soon as I don't get with that nigga pickles he gonna go back to her ass.I'm telling you don't make that girl your woman.the doorbell rang it was my mom saying come here you want to go with me bobby asked can she go mom say yes.so we got in the car to go to the store to get some things for my moms store.when we got to the store.mom went in we stay in the car.hey bryon have you ever bust a nut.what's that.that's white stuff that comes out your dick and it's called sperm.so if you put on the condom that bitch can't come and say you got her pregrant.when we got home I ran in the bathroom and took my dick out and it was white stuff on it. I washed it off and went out the bathroom.went to go tell bobby she was right but when I got up their her boyfriend Richard was there.me and Richard was cool. He had just moved around here and we use to go to parties together.he's the one that start me drinking. his brother Erick, was my age, Richard was bobby age.Richard use to throw the house parties,and since I was bobby's cousin he use to let me in for free.man we use to have so much fun.Richard throws the best parties he had the black lights and everything.most of the time the parties would be at his house. if they weren't at his house they would be at scooter's house that's larry and terry's brother son their nephew.Richard was bobby main man no matter who bobby fucked with on the side.she always fucked with Richard.Richard turns to me and say I'm sorry to hear about your dad.thanks man,you alright yeah just taking it one day at a time.man if you need me just let me know. Hey bobby do you have any more joints left.I got two left you take one and I keep one.cuz I'm finna get down to business.alright cuz I'll see you later.I went back down stairs to smoke my joint,I went to my room but couldn't smoke there mom would smell it. So I walked around the block when I got back to the house I see bobby's mom june coming.I ran around the back to warn bobby look in the window and see bobby naked.banging on the window telling her june was coming.she gets dress and Richard slipped out back door with me.good looking out dog,june would have killed us.yeah nigga I owe you. one just make sure I keep getting in the parties,we walk around to the front Richard rings the bell like he is just getting there.june comes to the door like nigga what you want.is bobby here,bobby your hot-ass boyfriend.Richard went upstairs and I went in the house to watch tv the phone rang and it was terry letting me know he was back.what you doing ,nothing watching tv,you got any weed,yeah I got a joint you wanna smoke yeah I'll be right out.I'll come down to your house in one second.I got to his house and knocked.his sister Claire answered the door.Claire was a fine grown-ass woman and I knew not to say anything out of pocket to her.she would've kicked my ass and sent me home.come in.I walked in and went to the basement where terry was.man your sister show is fine.I gave terry the joint and he lit it we smoke and got high.what's been up with you nigga nothing just trying to keep it together before the funeral.Claire called me upstairs in the kitchen.sit down I want to talk to you. she said I'm sorry to hear about your dad.but you know you have to keep it together for your mom you know.wait a minute I have something for you.she come back in the kitchen and hand me some weed.I don't smoke. don't play with me I know you terry and larry smoke.just take it you need it.when I got back downstairs terry says what Claire want.she was just talking about I had to be a man now for my mom,and gave me some weed.I didn't know she knew I got high.yeah she knows she gives me weed all the time.so we rolled up and smoke.oh yeah let me tell you what happened to bobby.I was sitting on the porch and june comes riding up.Richard and bobby had went upstairs to get it on.I had to run up the back and tell them june was coming.Richard get dress and leave out the back with me like he had never been up there.man if june had caught them they would have been in a world of trouble.how you know they were getting down.because when I went to tell them june was coming.I looked in the window and saw them naked.I know you wanted some of that.no man that's my cousin.well I want me some shes not my cousin.pass the weed nigga.man guess who I fucked in bobby's house,who linda with does big-ass titties.hell no pam fine ass. man she rocked my world she got some good ass pussy.what pam pam from skate-city, yeah she came over my house and we when upstairs and smoke some weed and drank some beer with bobby and linda. it just happened.man if pickles find out he's gonna be mad.no man he's trying to fuck bobby.I don't believe you, ask bobby and linda man.see we went to skate city last weekend me and bobby. my mom gave me the car we ran into pickles and pam.when it was time to leave they ask me to drop them off at home but we ended up at the park getting high.bobby and pickles were in the back seat making out and pam told me that she always wanted me but she was with pickles.plus she said I was the only one of pickles friends that didn't come at her.we took it from there so again how was it.it was great better than great I busted my first nutt.you say you made her cum while you was cumming you're a bad motherfucker but I still don't believe you.okay when we get finish smoking were going down your house and ask bobby and linda's big tittie-ass and get the real deal.we got through smoking and went down to my house bobby and linda was already on the porch.hey bobby didn't I have that girl up your house.who that pam girl.that must was her first nut because she's acting like she's in love.told you nigga.tell him bobby but before bobby could say something linda had to open her big ass mouth and say this little nigga done bust his first nut now he thinks he's doing something.shut up linda with your big mouth ass you always got something to say.that ant the only thing that's big this pussy is big too.with your lil dick ass.bobby shut your girl up before I kick her ass.linda get off that bullshit you to old to be on that bull.you know my uncle dick just died,and if he was alive you wouldn't be on this porch acting like that.okay I'm sorry,don't say it to me say it to bryon.bryon im sorry here light this.terry and bobby was rolling up some more weed.I hit the joint and went in the house to see what my mother was doing.she was in the house looking at pictures of my father.she look up and said what was that on that front porch. It was just me and Linda acting like we had no sense. Boy you smell like reffa you smoke that stuff. No that was terry and Linda. I don't want you acting like that on that front porch. Boy doesn't lie to me. Yeah I was out there smoking to. You better not leave that front porch. She came on the porch and everybody tried to hide the weed, but she smelled it. Bobby looks out for your cousin and don't let him leave this porch I 'm going to bed. Alright she left. and went back in the house. We all knew she wasn't feeling good because she always had a smile on her face. Bobby went up stairs to tell her mom that she was going to stay downstairs with us. She come back I asked her what she said, she said yes. We finish smoking but it wasn't the same because my dad was always in the window or on the porch.

I was never going to see him again, so everybody went home and me and bobby went to my house, I went to my room and started crying because I never thought in a million years that he would die so soon on me and then I went to sleep. The next morning I got up and went in my mother's room, she was still sleep and so was bobby. I went back in my room and call Herrick's house to talk to Lisa but they were still at breakfast I had to call her back. I went back in my room and went to sleep, when I got up later she had called me, "hey baby what are you doing", "just chilling, are you coming back after the funeral I don't know it's up to my mother now it's two days before the funeral and family members are coming in from out of town some from Detroit, down south and all over the county I was just trying to keep my head together and being strong for my mother.

Now the house is full of muther fuckers my cousin's from out west and south is all in the house, it's like being in Herrick house again but the only one I would let go in my room was my cousin Tommy. Tommy was my fathers sister's son, me and him used to kick it some times. I would go out west and spend the night at their house. he was the only one I use to get along with, the rest of them I couldn't stand because it was like they didn't like me or wish they were me, because what ever I wanted I got from my mother and father but my father was deceased and it was just me and my mom and it started sinking in. tommy was about two or three years older then me but he was my aunt's youngest kid. I liked my aunt ruth she was a good lady and besides she was a preacher we use to go to her church some times and hear her preaching. I liked the way she used to do her thang. She didn't sugar coat the word of god she'll tell you just like it is no matter who you were and I like that about her even then at my young age I knew she meant business she was a true god fearing lady, so tommy came over to spend the night over my house we talked about how my father used to take us to the drive inn, fun town, and shit like that then he asked me about what gangs was around my house I told him BGDN and he told me what was around his house. The BG's was around his house I asked him what was the BG's he said the black gangsta and I told him that the black gangster disciples was over here, are they the same he said no but they sound the same I asked him was he a BG and he said yes and then asked me was I a BGDN I told him no cause I was to young but I was a lil disciple we laughted at the shit and then watched some tv and went to sleep cause the next day was my father's funeral and we had to get some sleep. The next morning bobby came down stairs to get me she didn't know tommy had spent the night come on cuz you know we got to get it on before we go to this funeral uncle tommy I didn't know you were over here well I'll see you in a minute hold up I thought we were going to get some weed I don't smoke weed what but she was looking at Tommy. Tommy not gonna say anything he smokes weed to. "No I don't smoke weed". So you don't smoke and bobby don't smoke so I'm going to get some for myself and don't anybody ask me for none okay. Tommy wait here I'll be back bobby come walk with me to get the weed but I don't smoke but you do now. You just want me to go with you "yeah" okay I can do that lets' go on our way to get the weed bobby told me she didn't want tommy to know she was smoking weed because he might tell auntie ruth, auntie ruth was bobby grandmother so it was cool with me you still not getting my weed bobby walk like I know youre not going to act like that with me she knew she was my best female cousin and I wouldn't do her like that. So we got the weed and stopped at terrry's house so we could smoke before we went back to the house we rang the bell and larry came to the door what's up ya'll, I'm sorry to hear about your father what time is the funeral it's tonight at 7 where's terry he's down stairs me and bobby went downstairs so we could smoke with terry what up man nothing hey what time is your dads funeral at 7 where is it. It does gonna be at my cousin's church on the west side give us the address so we can be there before you leave. Ok we started smoking we rolled about two or three joints and I kept the rest so that I and tommy could smoke when I went back to the house. I told bobby to come on you know I left tommy at the house so we went back to the house tommy was like damn you were gone a long time man don't trip come go in the basement so we can smoke this weed I don't. smoke weed man,bobby gone upstairs you don't have to lie to me.I really don't smoke. Well more for me, plus I need it more than you do.Ok I'll smoke a joint with you.Cool we smoked then went back in the house into my room.then my mother told me it was the phone it was lisa. Hi baby how are you doing.I know your dad's funeral is today,so I'm calling you to tell you keep your head up and be strong,I love you.Okay I'll be seeing you then. Pam calling on the other line with the same old shit.I wasn't thinking about them all I was thinking about this is the last time I was going to see my dad.how hard it was going to be for my mom. Time went by fast and it was finally here the funeral car (limo).I've never been in a limo it was freakin me out.nobody notice.we picked up larry and terry. the ride was long from the Westside to the southside.the car had tv's in it.we made it to the church. it was so many people I didn't even want to get out the car.the driver let my mom out first then terry and larry I just sat there.didn't want to see my dad in a coffin.only been to one other funeral and didn't want to see keysha in a coffin.after keysha's funeral I had nightmares for 2 weeks.terry and larry came back to the car to say come on man this your last time seeing your dad.when on in sat behind my mom she beck for me to sit with her.she knew I was scared.there's nothing to be scared of.look up at my dad felt weird because I knew it was no life in my dad.went I sat down with my friends and cried.the services starts everybodys crying.eulogy was done by my cousin.theirs a lot of preacher in the family.and the funeral was over got back to our house for the. repass was at the house.house full of people all night.feel good to know how love my dad was.heard it all day.when every body left went outside to smoke the two joints I had from early that day.couldn't even get high couldn't sleep stayed up all night watching tv. The next morning mama was coming in my room to get me up. But I was already up she say's you been up all night. I couldn't sleep; just get dress for what the burial what's that. That's when they put him in the ground and put dirt on him and cover him up. I don't want to go, you have to go don't you want to see him for the last time. Causes after this you want see him again. I don't want to but for you I'll go. Okay get dress, got on up and got dress. The limo came and picked us up.and drove us to the burial just thinking. That was my last time to see my dad. We went back to the car and drove home mom went to her room and lay down. She wasn't feeling good I asked her if she wanted me to open the store. She looked and said no. I just want to rest, can I go out for awhile. Yes don't be out long, so I walked down to terry house but he was already on the porch smoking weed. Bobby reed says what's up ill brother sorry to hear about your dad. You know we been friends for a lot of years you stay strong. Thank you how's rose doing, she's at home napping she didn't feel so good after the burial. He left with chop that's Larry and terry's other brother. Here comes Tony down the street. What you niggas up to want to smoke some weed. No man I'm all smoked out. Terry and Larry smoked with him. Man I just heard about your old man sorry to hear that. They got done and we went inside down in the basement until it got dark. Man I'm going to holla at yall later going to check on my mom. See you later man, alright when I got home mama was sitting on the porch with my grandmother. My cousin June was out there too she was still crying. She hugged me and said it's going to be alright.then she sat back down next to my grandma. Stop all that crying before you make yourself sick grandma told her. I went in the house to get her a glass of water I was going to sit with them but she was still crying. I takes her in the house to lay her down then went to tell grandma that's she is o.K.That I was going to sit with her until she fall's asleep. Grandma comes in and I ask are you staying the night she answered yes, and we both got ready for bed it's been a long day. The next morning mama was feeling better she fixed breakfast we eat and she opened the store but she asks when are you going back to the Herrick house. When I make sure you are alright. Boy I'm alright; I'll go back in a couple of days. A couple of days flew by and it was time to go back to the Herrick house. Mama didn't feel like taking me so she took me to the train station. On the train now I can think about Lisa and what she was doing. While I was gone Lisa called everyday to see how I was doing. When I got to my stop a staff person was there to pick me up. We put my things in the car and we arrived in the front of the Herrick house Lisa lilbit and john was standing out there for me. Got my things and gave Lisa a kiss and we went into the building. John helped me put my things away and we went back were the girls were. Lisa couldn't keep her hands or her lips off of me. She acted like I was the only boyfriend she ever had. But I was glad to know that she cared, so we kicked it until it was time for bed. The next morning we went to breakfast and everybody was glad to see me. They knew I knew how to have a good time. And keep everybody in good spirit. I just didn't feel like being a clown now. I was off to myself I was thinking a little bit off bases you know what I mean. Wasn't myself but I didn't let no one know what I was feeling, just acted normal. My thought wasn't getting any better, I just knew that things were going to get worse but I just tried to keep my head on a good level. After breakfast we had chores to do, one was to clean up the TV room so me and john got it done as fast as we could so we could go kick it with the girl's. It didn't take that long because we were the first ones finish, so we went to see if the girls were through with their chores, they weren't so we went outside to play some ball until they got finished. After they finished up they came outside and kicked it with us. We just walked around the outside of Herrick house and talked, Lisa asked me how I was feeling because she knew me and my dad was very close. I looked at her in her eyes and couldn't lie, man lisa I don't know what I'm going to do my whole world is fucked up now and I just want it to be alright but it's going to take some time. Lisa was like don't worry I'm here for you I'm going to help you get through this and she gave me a hug and kiss and the forehead. A week had went by and things started to get back to normal I had been talking to my mother and she was feeling better, I had got back used to the routine at Herrick house and thinking like everything was going to be alright, till that next week came. Now I'm going on my second week back at Herrick house I'm back in to the staff members called me to the phone it's for you I think it's your mother, hey mama it's not our mother it's your uncle Lawrence. What's up uncle Lawrence what happen are you over my mother's house and you want to talk to me no I got some bad new your mother passed away last night and we will be having her funeral next week and I'll be to get you some time this week okay, okay and I hung up the phone. Man I just got back to trying to put my life back together when my father died two weeks ago. Now my mother died what typ of shit is this I just went outside by myself and started crying all I keep saying was what I did wrong to have this happening to me. I thought it was fucked up when my father died now my mother I don't have nobody it's just me. Then I thought I'm next because there's nobody to take care of me so I must be next. All that night I just went into a thing didn't tare up the place or went crying my mind just cut off from the whole world, I couldn't here or see anybody I just went to the dorm and laid in my bed looking at the ceiling until the next day I got up that morning and didn't want to talk to no one not even Lisa or john I just sat at breakfat and ate my food then when I got finished I went back to the dorm and sat on my bed at that point I knew I had lost my mind cause I didn't give a fuck about anything. No weed no girl friend nothing it was just me and fuck the world because I knew I was goin to die next. It was just a matter of time two weeks three weeks four weeks fuck it, I'll be back with my mother and father I'll be alright then lisa sent me a not john gave it to me it said I'm sorry to hear about your mother but I'm still here for you but I can't help you if you don't talk to me I still love you but you keep blocking me out and I don't know what to do I can't help you if you don't let me. just talk to me I'll try my best to help you get through this if you let me love lisa so I got out of the bed and went to talk to her for a little while. Then it was time to go to bed so I told her I'll talk to you tomorrow and went to sleep the next day I was feeling a little better so I came to breakfast with a smile on my face cause I had a good dream about my mother and my father it was so real but waking up in Herrick house let me know it was just a dream but it made me feel a little better I sat down at breakfast but I wasn't that hungry so one of the staff member cam over and told me to get my stuff ready cause I would be leaving after breakfast to go to Chicago my uncle was going to pick me up at the train station so I went back to the dorm and packed my things before I left I went and talked to lisa to let her know I was going and that I would call her when I got to my uncle's house one of the staff member's took me to the train station before I left I gave lisa a kiss good bye. And then I got in the car she was sad but I told her I'll make it up to you when I cam back your coming back right yeah you're the only thing I got in this whole world now she waved good bye and we left for the train station. I put my stuff on the train and I was on my way back to Chicago last time I was on this train I was coming from my father's funeral now I'm on this train going to my mothers funeral man this train is bad luck for me so about two hours I made it to Chicago train station when I got off the train I thought about how would I know uncle Lawrence cause I have not seen him in a long time. As I said that I saw him looking just like my daddy when he was younger, Uncle Lawrence hey boy I didn't think you would know who I was you look just like my daddy when he was your age you look the same. Come on and we got in his car and went to his house I thought we were going to my house there is nobody at your house then it really kicked in. there was nobody at my house anymore I asked uncle Lawrence, could I have some money so I can go by my old house for the last time, he said yes and gave me money so I could go to my old hood after I unpacked my things after put my stuff up I went in the kitchen to get something to eat, my uncle Lawrence wife cooked you washed your hands boy yes mame okay you can eat I got done with it so I could go to my old hood. I took the 95th bus to the train and the train to 55th street bus east to laflin and walked to 56th when I got on the block I stopped at Larry and terry house to see if they were home Larry wasn't there but terry was gone. Hey whats up man I was just thinking about you sorry to hear about your mother man were were just kicking it two days ago I was asking her when were you coming back home and she said in about a week she was right but man I didn't want to see you like this are you doing alright I'm okay but this is the most fucked up year of my life my father died on one week and two weeks later my mother. Man I'm trying to keep my head up and not lose my mind but it's hard so who are you staying with bobby and June. No I'm at my uncle house now but I've been in a group home for the last three months its okay but I want to be around here. Hey I'll talk to Clair and my dad and see if you can stay with us. You talk to your people and see what they say okay I got some weed and he gave me a joint I smoked it and he went to get me some beer I could always count on terry and larry thay where my best friendes. So after we got through we went down to my old house and sat on the porch it wasn't no body on the block that shit tripped me out and it wasn't late it was about 8 pm.larry had some more weed so we smoked about two or three more joints then bobby came down stairs. Whats up cuz sorry about aunt roe roe bobby what happened she was doing alright the first week you were gone she opened the store back up and was doing what she always do, then I seen her looking kinda strange she started talking about you saying how she don't want to leave you but she got to be with him I thought she was going crazy but she knew what she was talking about I told my momma that I think aunt roe roe is crazy she told me she's not going crazy I think she is going to die cause she don't want to live in this world without uncle dick. Then the next dayshe went to the hospital and a day later she passed. Man that's some tuff shit but all she kept saying I don't want to leave my baby I don't want to leave my baby but I got to be with my man aut roe roe didn't want to leave you but she had to be with uncle dick do you believe that. Yeah because I knew how long they had been together over 26 years man I knew I shouldn't went back to Herrick house, she might still be a live. Don't blame yourself aunt roe roe just wanted to be with uncle dick and she has no pain she in a better place now she at peace, boy by the way where are you staying at. Uncle Lawrence house out south so is that where you going to be living. Not I'm just there for the funeral then I'm going back to the group home. What group home? Ive been at a group home for the past three months Herrick house wehre is it at. In barlett ill, where's that at. Far away from herei'm going to talk to june and see if you could stay with us she might let you stay with us cause you were uncle dicks son man It's cool I just want to go to the funeral and not try to lose my mind I'm only 14 years old and the way things are going now I don't think I'm going to make it to 15. Stop talking like that your going to make it to 15, 16,17, and some bobby I don't know I hope so but right now It don't look good hey larry walk with me to the bus stop alright boddy do you want to walk us I'm waiting for Richard. Here he comes hey Richard walked with us to the bus stop hey man you alright I'm okay for now man if you need anything just tell bobby and I'll see what I can do alright when we got to the bus stop Richard and bobby went back to the house larry stayed with me till the bus came. Call me when you get to your uncle house to let me know you made it there. Alright okay later I sat on the bus thinking about what bobby said and I think she was right my momm love my daddy so much she couldn't live without him and that's some deep shit I thought about that all the way to uncle Lawrence house when I got there my cousin laurie opened the door she was my uncle's daughter, laurie was abut three or four year's older than me but we use to get alone she was laid back cool not like bobby bobby was really cool and laurie was only child cool it's something about a only child makes you look at things from another point of view me and laurie all ways got along cause my dad and her dad were close. My dad was the oldest out of his brothers and sisters and Uncle Lawrence was the youngest he used to come and get me to come over his house and play pool with him and baseball and basketball he was my coolest uncle. But my uncle judge was the crazy man in the world but I loved him to death. He used to drink and drive all of them insane cause he stay on some bullshit that's the way I all ways love to see him he'll allways kick it off for me to laugh and sometimes he come tell me before he kick it off. He and my uncle book were the funniest men in the world to me. For six years up until I was about 10 they used to keep me laughing, uncle judge would say something to uncle book and book would cuss him out, then uncle judge would cuss him out and then they would act like they were going to fight and it would be the funniest shit you had ever seen in your life. I and Laurie sat in the kitchen talking because we all ways caught them in the act from the beginning to the end. Laurie asked me if I still knew how to dance I said yeah and we went in the basement to play some records and showed her some moves she had rogers grate vince it was a good record to dance to. It had that brake dancing beat and I showed her some moves that I knew how to do tell it was all most time to go to bed she went up stairs and got my uncle and my aunt come see this bryon know how to do that break dance move. They came down stairs to check me out and we had a good time then I thought about I had to call Terry and let him know I made it to my uncle house. Uncle Lawrence I got to call my friend to let him know I made it here he said okay and I called larry, larry I made it you just getting there, no we were kicking it and I almost forgot cause man I thought something happened to you. Okay are you coming over here today you mean tomorrow no I mean today it's after 12 it's already the next day I see what my uncle said then I'll let you know okay. Okay later. The next morning my uncle Lawrence took me clothes shopping to get me something I could wear to the funeral he asked me about Herrick house and did I like it I said it's okay I told him about my girlfriend lisa and the things we do there and talk about all kind of things. that Was really on my mind what was going to happen to me after the funeral was over was I going back to stay in Herrick house for the rest of my life I didn't know what to think but I'll keep it to myself and just take it one day at a time. My mother's funeral wasn't going to be at a church it was at a funeral home and it was in two days so I kept trying to keep my mind off it but it keeps poping up in my head so I was trying to get things to do to keep from thinking about it. My cousin Laurie was going skating that night and I asked her if I could go she said cool if my father say you can. Go ask uncle Lawrence he said I could go the skating rink was down the street from their house and the skating rink was on 95th three blockes away so we walked to the skating rink it was me and my cousin and her boyfriend when we got in the rink Laurie and her boyfriend went off to do their thing and I was just trying to find some one to kick it with. I didn't know nobody in the skating rink so I was out there by myself it was a lot of girls in the skating rink but I wasn't; getting no action but I kept trying then this one girl asked me your not from around here are you. No I'm here with my cousin she lives around here where are you from 56th street. 56th street you are along way from home you better watch yourself these niggas up here will fuck you up if you don't know somebody I'm cool I'm with my cousin they know her alright you be cool now and she skated away. I went in the game room to play some games and it was like everybody was looking at me like I was from another planet or something so I played two or three games and just left and went back to skating but I could still feel people looking at me so I went and found laurie and her boyfriend and told them what was going on she looked at me and laughed boy don't nobody in here want to do nothing to you I said alright and kept my eyes open cause I knew what I was talking about then that girl I was talking to came over by me I told you look out for these niggas there over there right now talking about you what did they say they want to fuck you up what cause you are not from around here your playing right, no I'm just telling you cause you seem to be cool to me but them niggas allways on some bull shit. Watch your back and she skated off again I went and told laurie what the girl told me she said it was about six or seven niggas and laurie went up to them hey ya'll this is my cousin they were like whats up don't be fucking with him we weren't going to fuck with him laurie we just didn't know who he was up here with come on ya'll so I went back to skating and that same girl came back again hey wants up them niggas still talking about kicking your ass my cousin talked to them its cool, no it's not them niggas said fuck what laurie talking about when skating is over they are going to kick your ass and it aint shit she can do about it or she will get her ass beat too I asked her what time was skating over she said about 12 so at 11:45 I was getting my shit and hitting the door cause I know what we use to do to niggas at skate city and I wasn't going to be on the other end of the beat down so it was 11:45 I grabed my sit and hit the door plus they were letting out early I hid by these two cars they came out looking for me but it was to late I was gone I could see them but they couldn't see me. Laurie and her boyfriend came out looking for me and asked them if they seen me, no cause if we seen me we'll be kicking his ass right now. For what you don't even know him. That's cause we don't know him he shouldn't have been around here he's not one of us. So fuck him like I'm going to let you do something to him you'll just get your assk kicked with his come on act like he's here no I'm not going to fight you cause your man's girl but you come back up here with that nigga I'm going to kick his ass and your's if you got something to say her boyfriend grabbed her and walked away. She started going off on him I'm glad my cousin did leave cause your ass letting that nigga talk any type of way to me and you didn't say shit you'll let that nigga kick my ass wouldn't you, you a punk ass nigga I hope my cousin all right then I broke down the block and sat on her porch until she walked up how long have you been sitting here, not long you were right them niggas was on some bull shit with you for nothing at all just because they didn't know you man fuck this nigga acting like he was with them niggas cuz. All yeah it's over nigga don't call my house and don't come over here with your punk ass and she slammed the door in his face. Man I can't believe this nigga would do some bull shit like that you know the boy that was talking when I said don't be messing with my cousin he go to school with me and he like me I should have been talking to him instead of that punk mother fucker I'm glad you did leave cause they were out there deep looking for your ass I was out there I could see them but they couldn't see me I seen you when you went off on that nigga and tried to fight I don't care if he would have hit you we bothe had to get our ass kicked cause I was coming to help you that's real she laughed at me and we both went to bed. The next morning she told me she wanted me to go to the mall with her and I did she drove my uncle's car she asked me if I knew how to drive I told her yes and she pulled over and let me drive we went to this mall called evergreen plaza she was not buying shit she was on some trying to find her a new boyfriend but I didn't care I was just glad to be out the house and have some thing to do to keep my mind off the funeral until tomorrow. She went to three or four stores before she found some thing she liked after she got through we were just kicking it in the mall walking around talking until it was time for us to go home she asked me if I had a girlfriend and I told her about Lisa and she asked what she was like. She's a cool girl and sexy you know what do she look like all she pretty and have's long hair and a sexy body do you like black girls I like all types of girls just as long as they look good have you ever went with a white girl yeah I went with one before all right but they have little pussy's what do you mean this one white girl I was with we had sex and she started bleeding it freaked me out I thought she broke my dick and I was bleeding but it was her pussy That was bleeding she told her mother and her mother told my mother and they got in my ass about it so I didn't juice another white girl since then my cousin laurie laughed at me and said she must have been on her period or she was a virgin whats a period its come's once a month it happens so women can have babys how old was she about 9 cuz I was 10 no she wasn't on her period she was a virgin and you broke her in so what your saying you were her first her frist what black guy no her frist dick in her pussy all that's what you mean I get it cause I thought all white girls pussy was to little cause they were white. Boy pussy is just pussy black, white or what ever it's all the same it's just pussy buy the way are you becoming wet what? do you bust nuts all yeah I bust nuts bobby put me up on that our cousin yeah you been fucking our cousin bobby no she put me up on what a nut was all ok cause I was just gonna say I don't give a fuck what the hell you been doing as cousin you get no pussy here come on you don't know some cousins be freaking each other o boy you got a lot to learn I never hord of that see this girl I know who I go to school with was likeing this boy right and then she found out that was his cousin so she used to go over his house and he use to go over her house so one day she was over his house and nobody was home but him and her and they were talking she told him how she use to like him before she found out that she was his cousin he said he used to like her too, before he found out they were cousins so they laughed it off for a minute when the next thing you know they were kissing and going at it before she knew it she said hey were fucking the shit out of each other and she was loving every minute of it she told you that yeah why she's my best friend and I told her I wouldn't tell but you told me you don't know her you right so what happened after that she put her clothes on and left his house and they been going at it ever since. Do people know that they be doing that shit, no she got a boyfriend and he got a girlfriend but when they are not with them it be going down and don't let one of their mother's or fathers go out of town cause all the time they are out of town they let them spend the night over each others house so they don't got any brothers or sisters no both of them are only childs that why their mothers let them spend the night so much time together cause they have no other childen man that's some deep shit that's not all of it. she thought on time she was pregnant and she didn't know if it was her boyfriends or her cousins baby so she went and got an obortion whats that when you don't want to have a baby you have an abortion you go to the doctor and the doctor take the baby out of you and what do they do with the baby I don't know what they do with the baby but they take it out of you man that shit's deep so did she ever tell her boyfriend. Boy don't be stupid how could you tell your boyfriend that you just had an abortion cause you didn't know if the baby was his or your cousins how in the hell can you tell somebody that's crazy. Yeah you right cause everybody would know then she was fucking on her cousin but is she still kicking it with him not like she use to she be with her boyfriend more than him I know when she told you that your mouth was on the floor no I wasn't like that cause she's my girl me and her been friends since we were in third grade so she tell me everything and I tell her everything like what none of your fucking business. Okay you don't have to go off on me and get mad I'm just fucking with you, its cool having you hear to talk to but I'm still sorry about your mother cause I liked aunt roe roe she use to be so cool every time she use to bring you over here she use to bring a lot of candy that way you used to like her no she used to talk to me and tell me things to make me feel good and I could call her ask her anything and she would tell my mother man I'm going to miss her I'm going to miss her too cause she was the best mother in the world a kid like me could have and she spoiled me I know she bought you a car at 12 man my father gave me everything but a car was out of the zone man lets go to sleep cause we got a big day tomorrow see you in the morning and we went to sleep. The next day came and I was up with the birds ready to get this day over with cause I knew I wasn't ever going to see my mother again and this was the third funeral I had ever been too the first was this girl who I went to school with and I couldn't sleep for days then my father and now my mothers funeral. I just learned about death at kesha funeral and now it was all around me but if you ask me kasha funeral who would be dying next I would have said me before I would say my mother and father cause I all ways thought I would go before them but I'm just a kid, kids don't think about dying it's to much other shit on our minds like girls new bikes toys not this shit I knew after they put my momma in the ground I was a kid no more it was just me and I had to do what I had to do then I asked myself what am I going to do and I had no Idea we got to the funeral home it wasn't a lot of people like at my fathers funeral it was my grandmothers the lady who gave birth to me jean and some other family members but I was happy to see terry at the funeral cause I really needed some one to talk to who really understood me and what I was going through cause most of my family was full of shit who didn't really like me some uncle's who didn't give a fuck about me cause of my dad and now he was gone and my mother was gond I knew I had no more family cause when they were alive everybody wanted to be in my place but now no one wants to be in my shoes I'm looking at all these fake ass people thinking to myself a lot of these mother fuckers my mother cant stand and some of them she use to love like terry she use to love terry cause he use to allways look out for me like a big brother my mommas sister whos' really my grandmother they love each other the lady who gave birth to me cause now I realize jean was never my mother she just gave birth to me and gave me to a real women who's funeral is today my real mother when I was younger I use to want to live with jean but now I just want to choke the shit out of her ass she died in place of my mother cause the lady in that casket is my mother from my birth up to my 14 years of living she took care of me till the day she died and there is nothing I can do to bring her back and I miss her all ready terry could see it in my eyes and he pulled me to the side hey man lets go outside and smoke this joint it'll make you feel better so we went outside to smoke a joint the funeral hadn't started so we went on the side of the funeral home to get our smoke on soon as we started smoking june and bobby came they had just got there I thought june was going to go off on me cause I was out side the funeral home smoking joints but she just came up to me and gave me a hug and said she love me and hit the joint she never ever did that she was always in my ass but I knew she was feeling my pain she was feeling it too cause my father was her number one uncle and my mother was her number one aunt that's why she moved up stairs from us so she could be close to them bobby stayed outside with us but june and clyde went inside I couldn't believe this shit was happening it was like this was a movie or something it just didn't seem real we got through smoking the joint and went in the funeral home I sat at the front of the funeral home looking at the casket I wanted her to get out and say I was just playing we can go home now but it was to real I just kept looking at her I couldn't cry something woulding let me I wanted to but I couldn't I was just getting mad and I didn't know why so I went in the bath room then terry came in there you all right no man I aint all right I can't take it you want to go out side and smoke another joint yeah we can smoke right here in here hell yeah in here this aint no church this is a funeral home so we rolled up three joints and started smoking I guess you could smell it cause the guy who use to live next door came in to the washroom man you can smell that shit all through the place so I don't care that's my mother laying up there no nobody just mine okay man I feel you let me hit the joint and I'm out I knew they smelled the weed but I didn't care about shit the only lady who loved me in the world was gone and I didn't want to here shit from anybody and they knew it cause nobody said a word but the preacher then I told him how I felt and he shut up and went back to preaching then my grand mother came and took me outside to talk to me you know she wouldn't let you act like that but she's gone and these fake ass people who didn't like her when she was here acting like they care if I had a gun I'll go in there and shoot all their asses. Me too? No I love you.

Just they fake ass muther fuckers in there. Then Terry came outside, "man just be cool, come on lets smoke another joint". My grand mother asked Terry would he stay outside with me and he said that's why he came out to try to keep me cool. Then my uncle Lawrence came outside to talk to me, he was the only one I would listen to. He calmed me down and then I went back in and kissed my mother on the forehead and sat down, everybody at the funeral was looking at me like I was crazy but I didn't care. I was looking at the casket and getting madder and madder, why did this have to happen to me, what did I do so bad that my mother and father had to die and leave me here alone. I kept asked myself then the funeral was over and I went back to uncle Lawrence house the repast was at our old house and I didn't want to go so uncle Lawrence didn't make me I just went in the guest room and went to sleep and got up later that night and asked uncle Lawrence when was he taking me back to Herrick house you want to go back all ready. Yeah I'll go back tomorrow because I don't want to be in anybody's way you're not in anybody's way stay two or three days then go back no I just want to go home cause that's the only home I got and I'll feel better when I leave and he said ok plus I wanted to see Lisa I went in the guest room and went to sleep the next morning I packed my shit up and waited for my uncle Lawrence to come back with my train ticket I just sat in the room and watched TV. After a while uncle Lawrence came back and told me my train leaves at 4:45pm and it's was just making noon so I took a nap until it was all most time to go I got back up at about 3:00pm uncle Lawrence told me if I wanted to I could still wait for a couple of days if I wanted to but I said no and told him I wanted to see my girlfriend he said that's why you're in a rush to get back you want to be with your girl yeah well I understand come on it's time to get you down to the train station you got to be there before the time on your ticket so we got in the car and headed for the train station on our way to the train station my uncle stopped and got us something to eat and he asked me if I want something to take on the train with me I got some snacks and we were on our way it didn't take long to get to the train station when we got there he looked like he didn't want to see me leave and he told me you got my number if you ever want to come and spend a weekend with us just call okay. so then he gave me a hug then I got on the train now I'm back on this bad luck train every time I get on this train I was going or coming from a funeral but I knew this was the last time I'll be getting on this train cause it was no body left but me living in my family. This was my last trip on this train cause I knew if I died I wasn't going to be riding the train back to Chicago I just sat there thinking what was next for me no more mother or father no more house or car it was a long and lonely ride back to Herrick house when we got to my stop and I got off the train it was a while before somebody came to get me from the group home because they forgot I was at the train station tell I called them then one of the staff member's came and picked me up when I got back to Herrick house it was bed time so I just put my stuff up and went to bed the next morning when I got up it was a lot of new people at the group home they must have came when I was gone to the funeral it was three new girls and two new boys my old friend's were still there my girlfriend Lisa her girl lil bit and my boy John they were happy to see me we sat down to eat breakfast and kicked the Bo Bo's. then john told me he was leaving and I asked where he was going he said independent living I asked what is that it's when they give you your own house and they help you pay your bills and get you a job man that's cool so when are you leaving in about two weeks are you taking lil bit with you. I wish I could but she'll be coming to see me on her passes that nigga was on ten and I was happy for him but I was going to miss him so we kicked it for the rest of that day until it was time to go to bed, we kissed the girls good night and went back to our side of the mansion to our dorms me and John sat up till morning kicking it about his new house he was telling me how he was going to have so many girls over his house and how I could come over any time and kick it with him we talked until we fell asleep the next morning when we got up for breakfast they came to get John to take him to look at his new aptment so I went to breakfast by myself. I sat with the girls and told them where John was and ill bit had her mind made up when John leave she was going to leave to. She said when he leave I'm running away to be with my man I thought that was cool she wanted to be with him that much I seen nothing wrong with that so we talked about it until breakfast was over and went and got ready for school I had two classes with Lisa and one class with lil bit so when we were in school the class we had together we use to kick it the last class I had was the one I had with lil bit so we didn't have that much work to do so after we got done with our work we started talking I was telling her I thought that it was cool for her to run off and be with her man she said she got to do it cause she wasn't going to be like Lisa when I was gone and ask her what did she mean by that she didn't tell you. No what? Don't tell her I told you "tell me" hold on John didn't say nothing to you no? He said he was.man I don't believe it you know that new boy Steve? Yeah she was kicking it with him but she told him about you what do you mean she was kicking with him you know smoking with us and going to the ole school spot with us so she was fucking him too they didn't fuck but she did kiss him and grinned that's all I need to know don't say nothing then she'll know I told you okay I'm not going to say nothing but I'm glad you told me I can't believe it while I'm at my mother's funeral she's out here getting her freak on. The last bell had sounded and it was time to go to the dorm so as I came out of class what did I see her talking to Steve and I walked right over there what up hey baby this is Steve did you meet him. No but he in our dorm room what up man I'm Steve hey I'm Bryon talk to you later Lisa I didn't say anything to her about I Knew she was messing around with him while I was gone cause I told lil bit I wasn't I just kept it to myself and give her a kiss like nothing was wrong but I was mad as hell but I kept my cool and played it off I wasn't just mad at her I was mad at John too for not telling me cause he was my boy so I couldn't wait for him to get back from looking at his new place so I could tell his ass off. We went back to the dorm and Steve came over to talk to me I acted friendly with him how do you like Herrick house he said it's okay it was better then the other group home he'd been in he said about six why? cause he used to get in to fights a lot so they moved him around I told him he didn't have to worry about that here I know cause they know better plus at the other group home's there are no girls yeah that's why you were fighting there was nothing for you to do but fight he laughed and gave me five and we talked for a while till John came back hey I see you met my boy Steve yeah he's cool I told you when he came back you would get along why wouldn't we nothing all John I got to talk to you okay just let me put this stuff up and I'll be back he went to put up his papers and came right back Steve let me talk to him alone for one minute okay so Steve said cool and went in the TV room man I'm madder then a muther fucker at you for what why didn't you tell me that Lisa was fucking with Steve when I was gone who told you Steve no who Lisa no how did you find out it don't matter how I found out I thought you was my boy you was the one who was supposed to tell me but that's cool I see how it is now no man it's not like that she didn't give him any pussy or nothing like that so it wasn't a big thing man come on if I was gone a week and they were kissing and grinding so if I was gone for two weeks they would have been fucking and you wouldn't have told me shit man it's not like that men just for get it cause you know if that was lil bit I would have came to you soon as you came back but you didn't give me a chance to. Soon as you got back I had just got my independent living papers so I was so happy about that I didn't get a chance to tell you about nothing else that's right so are we still cool. Yeah man so what are you going to do she don't know I know so I'm going to play it cool and see if she is going to tell me. Does he know you know about them? No. so Steve don't know no that's cool just sit back and see what they up to. You know it so how did it go at your new house it was cool it's not a house it's an apartment but I have my own shit so that's cool Steve came back in the room are you through talking yeah man come on hey did you get some weed while you were at your mothers funeral no I wasn't thinking about bringing any back cause I was so fucked up about my mother man I couldn't think to go get some weed and I need some right now. Hey man when we go skating tonight it's a guy who I know sell'es weed at the skating rink that's cool because I got some money and wouldn't mind smoking so when we go skating dont let me forget okay? Cool. Cool and then we went to dinner we sat at our spot where we always sat in but this time Steve was sitting with us and when the girls came to sit with us Lisa sat across from Steve and not me so I played it off like I didn't notice that and she didn't pay it any mind but john picked up on it and said something what's up Lisa you sitting across from Steve and not my man what's up with that no I just came an sat down I thought I was sitting in front of him yeah right you know how we do this so she got in the set that was next to her that was in front of me and we said grace and began eating I asked Steve did he find a girlfriend yet and everybody at the table almost chocked but me and john laughing it was our inside joke he said no and we kept on talking so I asked what kind of girl was he looking for he said nice looking nice body and cool to hang with man I know a girl like that he said who and I said Lisa he looked at me like I was crazy man that's your girl I know but she is all the things you said right or wrong you're right okay I'm going to find you a girl like Lisa so we can all kick it before my boy leave okay hey man that's cool what time are we going skating about 8:00 man it's been a whole week since I been in our old school spot hey Steve have you been to the old school spot no what's that its where we take the girls to be alone and do our thing you know. All man put me up on that? I will soon as you get you a girl I got you and that's our weed smoking spot to so we get down wrong in there it's the cooles' spot in herrick house I can't wait to see it I just bet you would? and I looked at John and we went back to eating after dinner we have about a half hour before we can do what we want to so I just kept talking to steve to see where his head was he wasn't to bright and I liked that cause he had no idea why I was kicking it with him but john knew what I was on and I played it to the tee it was time that we could leave the dorm so me john my new friend steve went to kick it with the girls lisa and lil bit and they brought a new girl with them name shawn she was a black girl about our age and she look all right I never met her cause she was new she had just got there while I was at my mothers funeral so the girls met us at our meeting place the game room we went in played two or three games of pool and some records and then we broke out to the back of the mansion till it was time to go skating I was still keeping my cool cause it wasn't time to bust them out yet so we went down by the lake to kick it was right behind the masion me and john took steve away from the girls and asked him if he liked shawn he said she was alright but he didn't know if she liked him so we told him we could hook him up and he told us to go for it so we walked back over there where the girls were and started talking hey shawn my boy like you who, who you think you know I go with lisa and you know john go with lil bit who you think steve all yeah why don't he talk for his self steve I think you look nice and I wish you were my girl man that's all you got to say come better then that come here and lets go talk alone so they walked off together and the rest of us gave them their time alone and talked amoung ourselves johned asked me if I was still going to buy the weed and I said yes cause it was all most time to go skating do you have the money on you no it's at the dorm come go with me to get it as we walked back to the mansion to go get the money john was tripping on me about how I was so cool and not going off about lisa and steve I told him it was not time when the time was right I was going to let them have it don't wait until im gone and then you go off do it before I leave man you know it have to go down before you leave cause the way I'm going to do it you got to see it trust me like butter like butter baby and we went to go get the money as soon as we came out it was time to go skating we got the girls and jumped in the van. The skaing rink wasn't to far from herrick house so it didn't take long to get there and we just couldn't wait to get the weed and I seen a store not to far from the skating rink I asked john did he bring his skates he said yeah good cause where going to put some beer in the case cool and it was on we skated for about an hour before john's man came threw. It was this older guy named david he sold us the weedd and we asked him could he get us some beer he said yes and went to the store it took him a long time and I thought he ran off with my money but john said he wasn't like that soon as john said that he came back with the beer and we put it in john skate case we couldn't wait to get back to herrick house so we could get it on so we skated one more hour and it was time to go back to herrick house we jumped out the van and ran to put our stuff up and went in back of the mansion the girls were all ready theere when we came out waiting for us to come out we rolled up the weed and we started smoking and drinking the beer it didn't take to long before we where high then a muther fucker just acting like fools the staff didn't all ways come out to the back of the mansion but I guess we were making too much noise so they came to see what was going on we hide the beer and started smoking cigaretts to cover up the weed smoke what's going on out here we were just kicking it why are you making so much noise we just got back from skating and we just had to much fun keep the noise down or your going to have to come in okay okay we'll keep it down and then they went back in herrick house so we cooled out cause we didn't want them coming back out there and blowing our high I asked steve if he was goning to get with shawn he said he was going to try so I asked him what was lisa going to say about that. he said what? I know you were messing with lisa before I came back but you didn't think I know about it lisa started talking what are you talking about you know what I'm talking bout when I went to my mothers funeral you were all up in his ass then I come back you act like nothing was wrong who told you this John no who don't worry about it is it true yes or no yes but I thought you wasn't coming back but I told him I was waiting for you how could you be waiting for me fucking with him we didn't juice or nothing you were kissing and grinning like you were you might as well then I looked at john he had a stupid look on his face and I laughed at him lil bit just put her head down and shawn was just in shock I had just dropped a bomb on all of them steve was trying to say I'm sorry to me lisa was trying to say sorry to me and shawn was like that's some bull shit and now your trying to get with me so if he didn't cocme back you would be kicking it with lisa what trype of shit is you on hell no I can't fuck with you you could have told me you used to fuck with her I didn't so what do you call it man. Keeping her hot till I come back come on bryon lets get the fuck away from these assholes I'm not tripped in just had to let you know I'm not stupid and I knew all along lisa just put her head down and started crying I don't know why your crying you wasn't crying when you were getting your freak on with this nigga I'm not crying because of that I'm crying because I know your going to break up with me you got that right but I love you how could you love me and I'm not even gone two weeks and youre with sombody already man it cool I'm not going to cry fuck that lets get high john give me another joint and I started smoking lisa walked back to the masion and steve just looked at me and put his head down and shawn put her arm around me and told me it was going to be alright then steve walked off lil bit asked shawn to walk back with her shawn asked me was I cool I said yeah and she walked back with lil bit. I looked at john and he told me go ahead man it's just us here you can cry and I looked at him and laughed my ass off what the fuck are you talking about I told you I was going to getem and this was the right time before steve could hook up with shawn now I got her locked what? don't tell me your going after her you got it they tried to play me and they got played now he never hit but she still cheated right he had a chance to hit shawn but she don't want to fuck with him because of this so that leave me on top he didn't get to hit lisa when she was my girl and I took his new girl before he got to hit her now tell me aint that the shit. Give me five and another beer so we just sat out there kicking it till it was time to go to bed and then went back in the next morning went just like I thought it would me and shawn and lil bit sat at the same table with john and lisa and steve at at another table but not together and everytime I looked up lisa was looking at me but I would look at her I knew that this was getting to her so I kept it up and didn't look at her the whole time we were at breakfast until it was time to go to school then at school I just did my work,and still didn't look at her until it was time to change classes.we had two or three classes together.I knew it was getting to her because we use to talk to each other in every class to make time go by faster.but I wasn't going to give her chance to say shit.I sat on the other side of the classroom.always made sure someone was sitting between us make sure she could'nt say anything without the teacher seeing her talk.I would just keep my head down doing my work.every time I looked up she was looking at me I could feel her eyes pierce me but I kept my cool.but kept doing my work until it was time to go back to the dorm.when we went back to our last class she did'nt have that class with me.lilbit had her last class with me she sat next to me to tell me about how sorry her girl was,and she'll never do it again.I just listened to her talk,but lilbit you're the one that told me what was going on.yeah but I didn't think you were going to break up with her.I thought you would just hit her in the eye not stop fucking with her.thanks I'm glad you didn't tell her I'm the one who told you.for what cause she's still my friend.come on she doesn't want to be with no one but you. how could that be as soon as I leave she hooks up with steve.come on lilbit I know she's your girl,but dam it's not like I don't have feelings for her but she broke my heart by not telling me.acting like nothing happened.that's what really made me mad cause if she had came to me herself I would'nt be that mad but I had to here it from somebody else. But just give her chance to make it up to you.yeah I'll think about it.the bell rings and it time to go back to the dorm. Soon as I come out the class guess who Lisa talking to Steve. look at this lilbit see what I'm talking about I just walks off.lilbit walks over to lisa and go off on her.i'm taking up for you and you out here talking to this nigga.what the fuck is wrong with you.do you want to get back with your man or do you want this nigga.what is you talking about I was just talking about some school work.well you should be talking to your man about getting back with him not talking to the man you cheated with.it's not like that not like I've havent been trying to talk to him but he's been acting like an ass I cant talk to him right now.look lisa what you did to him.if he had did that to you what you would have done you'll do the same thing.i'll be acting the same way,just tell him I still love him and I want to get back together with him.lilbit told john to talk to me he did.but I knew what I was doing I was'nt going to get back with lisa until I got the chance to fuck shawn.shawn would'nt give me the time of day so I had to keep lisa out of the picture until I got a kiss or something from shawn. I wasn't going to give steve lead way so he could get up with lisa.so I had to make steve think that I was going to get back up with her,and make lisa think that we were not going to get back together. It was hard work but I had the both of them eating out the palm of my hand. I had steve trying to be my friend he knew john was leaving and nobody else liked him so he knew when john left he would be all alone.he did everything I told him to do. He did it and didn't give it a second thought. Whatever I didn't feel like doing I told him too do it when I didn't feel like doing schoolwork or clean up Steve was the perfect man for the job. The plan was moving so smooth I didn't have to do anything. the day was is coming soon that john was going to leave us the day before we had a party for him in the gameroom and we were going skating after the party was over.that night shawn wanted me to get up with her so I told her we wasn't going skating.while everybody was at skating we could get our fuck on and she was up with that.I told steve to pick up the weed and beer so we could get high with john before he leaves. Steve was like ok your not going skating with us.no but wake me up when you get back so we can get fucked up with john before he leaves.he sayed cool so I told john he had the money for the weed and drinks. he ask why arent you going skating.i told him I was going to bone shawn, but if anyone ask tell them I was sleepy and wanted to get some rest. So everybody believed him and went skating.it wasn't that many staff on duty that night so when they left for skating me and shawn went to our spot but when we got there staff was there they didn't see us.they took our made up beds we made. we went to the back of the building by the lake. i put her on the table and started to kiss her she had a dress on so it was easy to get to her panties.i pulled her panties down and put my dick in but it was so tight I asked her was she a virgin she said no but I thought she was so I took it easy and didn't do it so hard.we had sex for about thirty minutes before I busted a nut and I wanted to do it some more and so did shawn. We went back inside to see if some one was looking for us and thaey wasn't so we went and finished our business.went back inside to watch tv in the tv room.shawn got sleepy and went to bed I stayed in the tv room thinking about how good shawn's pussy was but not better than lisa's.then I got sleepy and started for my room then everybody busted in they were back.i'm all charged to get high but steve blew it trying to buy beer while at the rink and tried to roll a joint in the van and got caught he told them that he got it from me. Staff came in my room to question me they asked me where did I get it from I told them I got it when I went home for my mother's funeral.they didn't take me to jail but told me not to do it no more and let me out the car. Now I'm mad as hell this dumb motherfucker tricked on me,got my weed took I wanted to kick his ass but john stopped me.but he had some weed for me to smoke with him.i'm thinking this nigga not that dumb he did that to get me in trouble and kicked out the herrick house. So it wasn't time to go to bed so we kicked it until it was time to go to bed. The next morning I asked john did he think that steve got caught to get me in trouble.john said no he was trying to get some girls to like him and pulled the weed out in front of them and staff was watching him.he's just a dumb ass nigga.so what did the police say they just wanted to know where I got it from. I told them I got it when I went to my mom's funeral in the city. Good know we can smoke this weed so lets go and get high for the last time I'll be leaving in about four hours.so we went some where we clould get are smoke on I told him about me and shawn and we almost got busted by staff.how did they know about our spot somebody had to tell them cause they never comes to our spot. I think that nigga Steve told until he came they didn't know about the spot.now they know about everything the weed drinks everything. I think that nigga did that shit on purpose so we can get kicked out. I don't know about you but I don't trust that nigga.john said I'm going to ask him about this shit, so I said do you think he's going to tell you he's tricking on us. The only way we were going to find out if he's a trick is to set this nigga up. Tell him something made up and see if he's going to trick.yeah that will work. Let's make up something fast before you leave. I got it let's tell him we have a pound of weed and were going to be selling it just as soon as we bag it up. All we have to do is smoke two joints with him and tell him that's the weed were selling,and if the staff look for it we got his ass.yeah that'll work so tell him it's mine. John went in to find Steve to bring him out and I stayed outside john came out with Steve. I got it started hey steve did john tell you we got a pound of weed were selling.no he said just come smoke with him.well we got a pound of it and when it's gone I'm going to call john and get another one and were going to make alots of money.here hit this joint this is some of it and tell me how you like it. He hit the joint and said it was some good weed. So you'll buy some, hell yeah just let me know when you get it. Already got it, you mean to tell me you got a pound of this shit. Alright just get your money ready and I'll hook you up.okay just give me a little time don't trip.so let smoke this other joint because you know john is leaving today. So we just getting fucked up back here.steve finished and he left. I still had two joints I gave one to john and I kept one. John hurry up you know that lil nigga is going to trick.we finished and put some smell good on and went back in the building. Soon as we got back in the building what did we see staff searching.what are you looking for,you know what where looking for if I knew I would'nt be asking.so why don't you just tell me where it is, where what is?the weed we know all about it. A pound of it that you got. I look at john and he knew what I was looking at him. For, I could'nt do anything but laugh so hard me and john knew it was'nt no weed, I knew I was going to kick this lil niggas ass when I got the chance. Staff took me in the office and asked me all kinds of questions, where is it, where did you get it from do you want me to call the police.they were trying to scare me.so I went on told the truth me and john just made that up to see if he was a trick and he was one. Then they looked real stupid and tried to cover it up.we smell weed on you this isn't about me smelling like anything. The last time you caught him with weed not me he said it was mine and I took the fall for it.cause he was a punk and thought I was going to jail and I wasn't scared man my mother and father had just died not to long ago.do you think I give a fuck about going to jail I don't even give a fuck about living right now.they looked at me in my eyes and knew I was upset and knew I wasn't lying, and left me the fuck alone. I left the office and went back to my room soon as I got there john was finishing his packing. I told you that nigga was a trick. Yeah man you said he was a trick. So what are you going to do about it? Im going to kick that nigga's ass when I get the chance.i'm sorry you want be here to see it. But I'm going to kick his ass for the both of us. I'm going to miss you Man. but I can't wait to get my own crib. Man you need help with your stuff. Yeah men help me put my stuff in the van and I waited with him until he left. So I went back inside the building and it was time for lunch I went to the dining room to washed my hands and went sat down at the table.

here comes lilbit lisa and shawn it was all fucked up I thought lil bit was going to run away to be with john. I asked her I thought you were going to run away. She said that I'm going to wait, because they'll know where I'm at. Your Right.I look at Lisa and said Hey Lisa, oh you're talking to me sense your boy's gone. Well fuck it then I don't have to talk to you then.i'm just playing you know I miss talking to you. You still mad at me. No I got somebody else to be mad at right now. As soon as I said that Steve comes and trying to sit at our table.before I knew it I said nigga you know you cant sit your ass over here. Nigga first you tried to take my girl then you got my weed took then you tricked on me I don't fuck with no tricks so get your ass from over here.what happened, I'll tell you as soon as this nigga get his ass fron over here. Then Steve got up and left. First I sent his ass to go get some weed at the skating rink and he fucked that up then I thought he was trying to do that shit on purpose. That was your weed he had in the van. Yeah but wait so Im at the spot and here comes staff where they never come he had to tell that's.not the end of the story so I tell john what I was thinking and we sat his ass up. And told him we have a pound of weed and when we get back in the building staff was searching my things? And the killing part is he sat and smoke two joints with us before his trick ass go's and tell's on us. But what he didn't know was that we made that shit up just to see if his ass was a trick. He is and I don't fuck with any tricks. So we all made up that day where not fucking with Steve ass okay. Everybody says okay, so we were through with lunch and we all went behind the building were we always be hing. But it wasn't the same since john was gone. Yall wants to smoke I got some weed not no pound though john left me with a couple of joints. Hey lilbit when are you going to blow this popsicle stand. In a couple of days I;m giving his ass time to get the house together you think I'm going to be in here and my man out there doing what ever he wants. I feel you, nigga your ass is a fool.you smoking Lisa. Yeah I don't want your ass to be mad at me. Why would I get mad with you if you don't smoke moer for me? How about you Shawn yeah I need to relax. Don't we all I'm gonna kick that niggas ass? Who? Steve. Don't let that punk get next to you? The right time is going to come and I'm going to kick that ass for him. Why you didn't go skating with us last night. I needed to get some rest more than a good time. The Man john and you used to get your drinks we used him to get us some. And boy was I shit face last night. The last time I got shit face like that was when I was at home. So yall had a good time yeah we got good and high. I'm telling you should have been there. You know the skating rink got a new DJ he was playing all the good music we skated and dance and got fucked up. That's good I'm glad you had a good time. We gonna do it again and I'll be there. But it want be the same without john yeah you right but fuck it I'm going to make it the same I'm going to be john and me all night you got no sense but we love you man. Hey the weed is all most gone. We have one joint left so since its one joint left. we gonna let lilbit kick it off so I gave it to her. And she gave a speech to us. I'll light this joint up for my man that was giving to me by his best friend I hope it'll keep me high until I see him again. Girl light up the damm joint so we can get high.we finished getting high and went back inside. When we get inside a boy name Dave came up to me it tripped me out because he never came to me before. He says I know you need a sidekick since your boy is gone and you don't fuck with Steve any more and I need to, get up with the girls and I want trick on you like that mark ass nigga Steve done. So think about it you don't have to tell me now. Your cool we can kick it so Dave became my new best friend. Plus Dave's family comes and sees him and gives him money so I knew I had to put him on my winning team. I asked him which girl did he like, he told me and so I knew I had to hook him up. It was lilbit he liked so I told lilbit and she looks at me like I was crazy. But john had played her to the curb so you know that she started talking to Dave after that but she wanted me to get back with Lisa because she didn't know that I was messing around with Shawn nobody knew but me and her. She was getting mad at me she wanted everybody to know and I didn't. I still wanted to do my thing with Lisa too but she knew I was on some bullshit so she stops fucking with me and tried to make me mad by messing with Steve. But she didn't know I didn't give a fuck anyway ,because I had got what I wanted anyway and I got back with who I wanted to be with in the first place, but I still wanted to kick his ass for tricking on me. But I had to wait for the right time but little did he know his time was coming sooner than he thought. Dave was a good sidekick we would go to the skating rink and he would buy the weed and drinks. The days that I didn't go he would still have my back when I was'nt around if he heard something that he thought I should know he would come and let me know like one time when the staff was watching me at the skating rink he came back and told me. So I would let him do what I was suppose to do Like get the weed and drinks. So let it be told he was a better friend than john. He kept me up on everything we were bestfriends now. But I knew something bad was about to happen because everything was going so smooth. Then that day came when Dave told me that Lisa was still fucking around with Steve because Shawn had told her that we had fucked around on the side and nobody knew but her and me. Dave had seen Lisa and Steve at the spot when he had went on the roof to hide our weed he saw Lisa and Steve go to the spot to get it on. So he told me and I knew he had no reason to lie. So I had planned to catch her in the act I wasn't going to go to her with no he say she say shit I was going to catch her ass. So we both kept it a secret I told him not to tell lilbit because she would tell Lisa that I knew. I had already put it in my mind what I was going to do and that was going to give me a reason to kick his ass for fucking with my girlfriend. So the staff could'nt kicks me out. That time had to come and I could'nt wait for them to try to go to the spot and get it on. But two or three weeks had passed and nothing had happened. Then came the fourth week had come and dave came running in the tv room where I was sitting come on man I think they are trying to make a move. So we jump up and run out the room and out to the other side of the building and went to the side were we could get to the roof. We got to the roof and we hear them talking. So what up Lisa you havent been missing around with me so whats going on. It's not like that I just didn't want to be caught and keeping it cool. But it's been four weeks nobody's watching us. So we better get it on now why we have a chance because we might not get another chance for a long time. Your right she looked around and they headed to our spot and Steve let the window up and they went for it. Soon as they went in me and dave jump off the roof and ran to the other side so we could look in. then she laid on the floor and took her pants off they started kissing then he got on top of her I could'nt wait for their asses to try to come out of that window. So Dave and I waited for them to get through. As soon as Lisa came out of that window I went off what the fuck are you doing. I was just talking to Steve I knew if you seen me talking to Steve you would go off. So we came to the spot to talk.tell the truth, ask him Steve tell him the truth so Steve comes out the window whats up. Tell him the truth were'nt we just talking about a problem I was having with my girl and she was telliing me what to do. Me and Dave were looking in the window and Dave did they just look like they were talking. No it didn't look like they talking it look like they were fucking to me. Me too then I hit steve right in the eye and started kicking his ass he didn't even hit me back he just let me kick his ass. Lisa just ran and Steve tried to run but I caught his ass in front of the building and kicked his ass some more. Then Lisa came out of the front of the building with staff. I thought you where a tough ass nigga your nothing but a bitch ass nigga. They made me stop I thought you where a tough ass nigga your bitch ass. Staff asked us what was we fighting for. Steve says I was fucking his girlfriend. Yeah yeah keep lying before I kick your ass some more take your ass in the building were your bitch ass is going to call the police. It was just a fight we don't have to call the police. No man you are going to jail fuck that. So we went in the building and they called the police and they came and got me. I got out the next day when I got back to the Herrick house they had my shit packed. I didn't know where they were about to send me so I asked. My caseworker told me that if they had'nt found some were by tonight they would have to take me to my aunt house. So I get on the phone and call terry.hey terry ask your dad if I can come to stay he says his dad said yes. They had known me all my life and besides they would get a check for me. I had to share a room with terry but I didn't care because terry was one of my bestfriends. So I looked at Lisa and said you make me sick you lil bitch it's your fault bitch. I packed my stuff and they took me to terry's house when I got there I went in and we kicked it. He asked me what had happened at the Herrick house I told him. And we kicked it until till it was time for bed because he had school the next day. The next day we went up to my old school bomtemp to get me in school thay would'nt let me back in their school. So terry dad said he would take me to gage park tomorrow to get me in school and I said cool. We went back to the house I was thinking that was cool im going to be in a highschool but I knew that was'nt going to happen because I was still in the 8th grade. So Bruce called the caseworker to get my school records and till she did that I didn't have to go to school. I just sat around the house everyday until terry and Larry got home.and help Claire keep the house clean I would get my smoke on. But I wanted to go to school so I could meet new girls and friends. So the day came that they got me back in school at bontemp and I was glad. Some of the same kids were from when I went there the last time and they remembered me. They asked if my mom was going to bring me stuff. Like when I was there last time. My answered would always's be no my mom and dad died they left me alone. Lots of the kids were scared of me because of the shit people was saying about me. Like I killed a teacher and I was half crazy but I didn't care I was glad to be home. I didn't want to live with my aunt and I was living with my bestfriend. Living with terry was cool but then it got ruff sometimes it was no food in the house. To think I always love to eat and wear new clothes but that wasn't happening. there was'nt any money I was really feeling it. Wishing sometimes I was back in the Herrick house. But I fucked that up; I still kept my head up. But my big brother Tarry kept me looking good for the chicks. One day a boy named wankie came up to me to ask if I wanted to make some money and I said yes how. He wanted me to break in somebody's house with him me looking at him like he was crazy. Thinking about no food or money I went alone with him. We case out two or three houses but people were there so I said I know a house. He said who, my cousin's house man you are not going to break in your cousin's house yeah man it's no food or money in the house. Plus they wouldn't let me stay with them when I didn't have no place else to go, and they have a lots of stuff two or three tv's, money and everything so if you don't help I'll do it by myself. Nigga be cool I'll help you do it. First let me talk to my nigga he's always with me when I do jobs like this. We got to this dude house he knocked on the door and this dude came out and theywent back in to talk then came back out. We went to my old house and rang the door bell to see if any body was home nobody came to the door. We walk around to the back I look in the window and the lights were out so I knew it was'nt anyone at home wankie tried to leff the window but it was locked. I'll go get a knife so we can open it. I went down to where I use to stay and find a knife. I went back upstairs give wankie the kniffe open it. Wankie open the window and we went inside and start to take shit we could sell TV's radio's things we could sell right away. I never did anything like this before never had a need to. But I Wanted wankie and dude to think I was cool and tough. So we got the stuff were taking and set it by the backdoor took one more look to see if we missed anything. I started to put the stuff in my old apartment that I stayed in. wankie was like man what the fuck are you doing that for let's take it to my house. We got to wankie's house he lived two or three blocks away. We sat in his house until he got this call from a guy that owned a pawn shop plus wankie had dealt with him before. Finally the call came for wankie and dude tells wankie he'll give us 6 hundred wankie said give us 6 fifty dude said cool he comes and pick up the stuff he payed and leaves. Wankie gives me 2 hundred and gives dude 2 twenty five, his guy was like why you didn't give him 1 fifty he wouldn't be happy with that.

No man he put me up on the lick and if it wasn't for him we would still be broke. Yeah you right you want to shoot dice hey kid you know how to shoot dice. No but you can show me. Okay it like this if you roll 7 or 11 on your first roll of the dice you win, if you roll 2 or 3 or 12 on the first roll you lose, and what other number you roll on your first roll is your point you have to roll that again to win. Ok what if you hit a five on the first roll, you got to roll a five before you roll a 7 or you lose you understand yeah. Come on lets play I'm first he rolled the dice and his point was a 6 his next roll he rolled a 6 again so he won.his next roll was a 10 but his next roll was a 7 so he lose. Now it was wankie's roll he rolled a 7 the first time and won. The next time that wankie rolled he craped out and it was my roll I hit a 7 on my first roll and won my next roll I won again and wankie was like you sure you have'nt played diced before. No this is my first time so I craped out and it was wankie's friendes' roll and he rolled a 12 and I said 12 is your point wankie says you won the dude got mad at wankie and said if this lil nigga don't know how to play you aint got to tell him. I'm not gonna let you cheat him. Im not trying to beat him he's the one that's winning I played two more times and I told them that I had to be in the house at 10. I gave wankie 5 and got the hell out of there before some bullshit broke out because I was feel that shit coming on so I left. I stop and got some weed and something to eat. When I got to the house terry was up he says were you getting some money from I told him and he looked at me like I was crazy. What's the fuck's wrong with you, you broke in your own people's house that's some dirty shit man what the fuck were you thinking man you need to get your shit together. Terry you are not going to tell on me. No I'm not going to do that but I had to let you know that was some real dirty shit you did. Hey I got some weed. Man I don't even want to smoke I'm going to bed. After terry went to bed I sat in the kitchen feeling real bad. That the only family that's around me and even though me and june didn't get alone me and my cousin bobbie where cool like sister's and brother's. That's the only thing that bothered me. I knew that if Bobbie ever found out that it was me she would be so mad at me. I felt like shit I just sat in the kitchen smoking on that joint feeling super bad. Then it hit me how bobby use to let me fuck girls in her room how she always smoke weed with me,going skating with me going to the park just having to much fun. But it really got deep because I started to think about my mom and dad at fourteen I was going through more stuff than a grown person trying to keep my head up and not just lose my mind and go completely crazy. It was like having the world on my shoulders at 14 kids were doing what kids do but I was'nt on that I was doing what grown people do. I didn't want to be breaking in nobodys house just to eat and be a bomb in the streets. I just wanted everything to go back like normal when life made sense I lived like a prince. The only kid driving to school. I wanted to know how I went from all that to having nothing. So I knew I had to deal with it so I just finished up smoking and went to bed. The next day after school I was coming home and I saw bobby she gave me a dirty look I asked her what was wrong. She said you know what the fuck is wrong you broke in my house and you are going to get your ass kick as soon as Dwayne comes around. So I went back to the house were I was staying and wrong the bell tracey came to the door were's terry ,he's in the basement I went down in the basement and said terry I thought you were'nt going to say nothing. I didn't what the hell you're talking about. So what the hell is bobby talking about? Shit I don't know man.then here comes Larry down the stairs what's this shit I hear about you broke into bobby's house. Who told you that shit bobby told me that old man larry and sonny was in your old apartment and heard you and saw you come out there backdoor with there shit. I forgot they were still living in the apartment. So you did do it that's on you I can't believe you could do that. Don't say nothing I feel bad as it is. Okay they did say it was dark outside but it sound like your voice. But they couldn't tell that it was you Bryon and plus bobby said that Dwayne is going to kick your ass on sight and you better hope June don't call the police on your ass. Cause you will go right to jail with no problem.

What made you do some shit like that. I was talking to that nigga wankie, that's all that nigga do is break in people's house. Don't be fucking around with that nigga unless you want to get your head blown off. He's broke in a lots of people house and it's people in the hood who's house he broke in the hood that wants to blow his head off. Stay away from him before he gets you killed. I didn't want to go outside so terry went to the store for me to get beer and weed. But he came back with bobby he was telling her that I didn't do it so she said ok. But I knew how she was she just wanted to smoke up the weed. I told her to tell Dwayne that I didn't do it and she said ok. But the next day I was going to this girl house that I met at school. As I was walking up the street I saw Dwayne and he tried to fight me so I ran and I ran right into Bruce. Bruce was Larry and tarry's cousin he could fight real good he saved my ass. Everybody knew that Bruce could really kick ass so Dwayne ran back down the street. As soon as I get to the house here comes the police to lock me up. They put me in the police car and rode me around asking me questions like who was with me we know you did it so tell us who was with you we know you're too young to be breaking in people's house. You don't want to go to jail do you? We know somebody put you up to it. I told them it wasn't me. So they rode me around some more thay seen some guys outside the store and one of the guy thay knew they call him up to the car he seen. Me and ask me what I did. They told him and ask him to talk to me did you break in to an aptment in the building that you use to live in. he ask could he talk to me alone they tell him yes. So the police let him get in and they went into the store. He says if you tell them who? Did it they will let you go. I don't want to be a trick, tell me and I'll tell them it was wankie. Boys if it was wankie in this car he'll trick on your ass so fast fuck wankie. So when the police came out the store he told them who did it, it was wankie they knew wankie because it wasn't his first time doing this. They let me go and billy walked me home. So as we were walking and talking I said now I have to watch out for wankie's ass. You don't have to worry about wankie's ass cause if he fucks with you I'll take care of his ass. He knows you're too young to be out here doing that kind of shit. Plus he's knows your mother and father he just want to send you off. Don't be fucking with that nigga now take your ass in the house. So I started walking down the street he said where you going he uses to live down the street from me. I live with Larry and Terries now ok get your ass in the house. Don't let me come back and see your ass on the block. Your not I've had enough trouble for one night. So I went in but I came back out and the first person I see was wankie ass. He calls my name and said hey lil nigga I want to talk to you. About what the police said somebody told them that I broke into your cousin's house you didn't say nothing did you. Hell no I didn't say nothing for real. I just had to ask because after you left I won all that niggas money and he started asking crazy and I had to kick his ass. So I thought that nigga told and I guess I was right. So I guess I have to go around here and kick this niggas ass again. Alright lil nigga you got some money, Na I'm broke alright and he left walking down the street. So I went back in the house because I didn't want to get into any trouble and I knew trouble was his name. Plus I didn't know what that nigga was up to. I went into the kitchen to get something to eat and just like before there was nothing in the kitchen. I called a girl that I know from school and asked her can I come over and kick it with her she said yes. So I went over to her house she lived on 58 and bishop and I lived on 56 and laflin I didn't want to run into wankie so I just walked down bishop until I got to her house. When I got there I rung the bell and her sister came to the door I asked was Liz at home. Yeah what's your name, slydog your name is not slydog your mama didn't name you slydog. Liz this boy is at the door for you. Talking about his name is slydog I think he's crazy. Girl let him in, why you playing with my sister your name anit no slydog. Girl his name is Bryon he a guy from school. She askes me why did I say my name was sly dog. So I told her that's what they call me, why they call you that, because we have a dance crew called the disco dogs and everybody name end with dog. So that what they call me around the house but at school they call me Bryon. So I hope you can dance if you're in a dance group. Put on some music and I'll show you. She put on some music we danced for about 2 hours and I was really getting hungry. So I asked her if they had something to eat she said boy go in the kitchen and get you something it's to much food in there. So I went in the kitchen and she was right made me think about when I was home with mom and dad we always had food boy how I miss my mom and dad. I made a lot of food they asked me was I going to take some home. I answered no I'm going to eat all of it so I eat and went back upstairs were Liz was. She was talking to her sister about me because she remembered me from bons temp when I first started there when my mom use to bring me lunch and when I could drive the car to school. Her sister's name was Linda she looked good but not butty than Liz. Liz was my age 14 Linda was13. She had a body of an 18 year old big titts and a real nice face. Lind's butt was bigger. They had a little sister that was about 6 or 7 years old name dee. She was a funny little girl keep me laughing talking about her two sisters until she makes them mad and they make her go to bed. I really enjoyed going to there house so Linda asked me to bring a friend the next time I came and I said ok. So the next day I went I took terry with me and he saw Liz and said man I hope that's for me. Then Linda came down stairs and I said that's for you. Linda this is my boy terry, he's like my brother.terry this is linda,its cool lets go upstairs we gets up upstairs when we got in there room terry askes linda do they smoke weed. Yeah but I does'nt have none. So me and terry left and went to the store to pick up drinks and weed. hey terry I don't have any money. That's cool I got you, you always looked out for me. So what do you think about Liz. She's fine ass hell with those big titts. Linda looks good too with that big ass butt. While we were walking to there house who do we run into but that nigga wankie. Just the lil nigga I want to see. He pulled me to the side and said hey man did you talk to the police. No man, you already asked me that shit. Don't keep asking me that shit no more. I don't want to piss you off man do you have any money. I got 20 dollars you can get 5 dollars until I come up. Thanks man you know how we get down. Be cool man hey terry take care of my lil man and you stay up. I could hear him telling does niggas he was with that I was cool. He is putting me up on licks. Terry asked me you're not scared of wankie are you. No I use to but I know your with me and you anit gonna let nothing jump off and he was'nt going to pull shit while your with me. You know I got your back I was just asking cause you checked that niggas ass that why he gave you that money. He didn't want you to pull no bullshit but I'm glad you told me because I'm gonna keep that nigga out my face. Don't worry hes not going to be in your face no time soon. When we made it to the girl's house they told us that Bruce was looking for us. So I called Bruce he said I got my uncles car yall want to ride with me. Hell yeah so we smoke two joints with Liz and Linda until Bruce made it to their house. Bruce came in when he got there and we smoke some joints with him. The girls asked him did he drink. Yeah but not while I'm driving. So Liz askes you got a car, no it's my uncle car but he let's me drive it from time to time. So that cools so we can go for a ride one day. So we got finished and left with bruce.as soon as we got in the car Bruce says who that girl is with does big ass titts. Oh that's my chick. Man she was acting like she wanted to be my chick. Bruce gets off that shit. Terry was laughing his ass off but I was getting mad. Man doesn't get mad at us because your girl acted like she wanted to give me some of that pussy. Man just hit the joint so I did and came to my senses Bruce didn't do me wrong he just came to pick us up to kick it with him. Besides me getting mad was not going to do me no good because I knew I could'nt kick Bruce's ass. But Bruce being the big cousin that he was said he wasn't going to come at my girl but if she comes at me that's a different story. Okay that's cool. So we just started talking about something else and getting high. Hey Bruce terry says we were going to the store and on the way back we ran into wankie and Bryon checked his ass. We tripped on that and rode around for awhile until it was time for Bruce to take the car back. He dropped us back off at Linda's house. They let us in and bruce took the car back and walked back around the girls house we let him in and he gave us some money on the weed we picked up while we were out. While we were sitting talking Liz asked Bruce was he a disco dog. He said no but I know all of them. Liz look at me and said I thought you were lying I thought you made it up. Why should I have to lie about something like that my shirt is at home? Then Lind had to put her two cents in it he did lay like he told us he had a car in the 6 grade. Terry says yeah he did use to drive to school. Told you I still think he's lying. So what happened to the car when my mom and dad died they took the car away from me. If I had a car and my mom and dad died nobody would have took my car. I was in the group home, so what happened to your mother's house. They gave that away too that's so messed up. I feel for you, where you live now. With terry and his family. That's cool you got somewhere to live that so messed up you had it and they took it all away. I would be mad at the world if I was you. It hurts sometimes when I walk by where I lived and it reminds me of my parents and all the good times we had there. Liz could feel my pain and start to talk about something eles. Before I brought the whole house down, Liz started asking Bruce how old was he and what school he went to. I could tell Liz liked him by the way she was looking and smiling. I just kept my cool like I didn't know what was going on listening drinking my beer. Linda was on some fast girl stuff she took terry into her room and they didn't come back so I knew what was going on with them. But if I could get Liz to myself it would be on. I tell Liz to go get me a beer she went down to get the beer. While she was gone I told Bruce im never going to be the player that he was if he didn't leave. He said okay as soon as Liz comes back. Liz comes back with the beer and says Bruce you want one. No I'm about to leave. To bad he told her I know you wanted to spend some time with him. She looked at me and laughs. I told her I'll walk him to the door. We both got up to walk him down stairs he's says you better get that pussy. I gave him five as he went out the door. When I get back upstairs liz was sitting on the bed I lean over and started kissing her lips was so smooth I started kissing her neck, she sure was getting hot I pulled her titts out went right to sucking. them I cant wait to tell bruce. She really was hot and told me to stop. She got up and went into the bathroom and come back naked. I started to take off my pants she begins to help. She lay down and we were taking care of the business. She says do you know how to eat pussy. My respond was no and we just kept on fucking. She says again eat my pussy so I told you I didn't know how. A knock on the door its terry hurry up we got to go there mother is on her way home. We finished and got ready to go. As we were leaving out the door terry was standing there kissing linda.oh you not going to give me a kiss Bryon. Yeah I kissed her and we left. As we walked home I asked him hey terry how was Linda she's cool you know what I mean is her pussy tight. Yeah man good and tight, hows liz man does big titts and pussy is super big you know I have been with a lots of girls for my age but none big and loose like liz's. She has the biggest pussy I have ever seen before in my life. But was it good. No it was to deep I could'nt hit the end of it. She must be fucking grown men. I guess we talked about it until we made it home. When we got home I wanted to tell Bruce so I went in the basement were he was. Guess what Bruce, what you got some of that pussy. Yeah man but she got a big ass pussy. What you mean it's to deep you can't even touch the sides of her pussy. Get the fuck out of here have she had a baby no well maybe she just came off her period. Period what's that, that when a girl bleed from her pussy every month. But after she dush it get back tight. Why I didn't know because you don't have a pussy with your young behind. That's why we like to talk to Bruce he's older and he new thing. And if he didn't know he didnt making up shit. We love him for that shit and plus he's our big cousin. The next day when I got to school and made it to my class and sat at my desk Liz came over to me and said don't tell nobody about last night that between me and you. She sat down at the desk next to mine time went by quick it was lunch time. I hated going to lunch now because it reminded me of when my mom would bring me lunch. So every time I get to lunch I was wishing she be standing down at the bottom of the stairs with my lunch in her hand. I knew she was dead but I still be wishing. When we got in the lunch room I went and sat by the window to look out while I eat Liz brings her tray over and also Linda came over too. She wasn't in our class but she had lunch the same time we did. We sat and eat our lunch and talked about what we did last night. Linda say today is Friday and we got the whole weekend to kick it were going to have some money to. So don't forget when you come over to bring terry to. I couldn't wait to school let out I had a smile on my face all day. When school was over I walked them home then I went home to get my stuff ready for tonight. So I called liz to see what time she wanted me to come over but linda picked up the phone and said you still coming over. Liz said come about nine my mom and dad will be gone about that time. Her and my dad goes out sometime when they get off they want be back until 1 or 2 sometimes stay out all night depending on how they feel. All yeah bring Bruce with you too. Okay then I hung up the phone. Terry comes in the house and I tell him whats up he's charged man they gonna get us high with there money. It didn't cross my mind why she was asking Bruce to come because he got us high last night. So man what time is Bruce getting home they want him to come too. Bruce get here about 7:30, that cool they don't want us to come until 9 anyway. I couldn't wait until Bruce got home so I could tell him the good news. I and terry went to the store to get us some beer and we ran into Bobbie she looks at me but this time not with hate. She says what's up cuz want to smoke a joint with me. When you get back from the store just ring the bell. Ok when we were on our way from the store I told terry I'm not going in June's house. I fell you man I would'nt go over there either. So we walked passed her house and she comes running out the building saying where you going you don't want to smoke with me. I said no you anit going to get me up there and let Dwayne beat my ass. No it's not like that I know that nigga wankie done it and the police got his black ass in jail. June told me to tell you to come over anytime you wanted too. Yeah right you don't believe me. She ran upstairs and got the phone to call June and handed me the phone. Hey I know you didn't break in my house and I'm sorry you can come over anytime you want to. The police told me you told them who done it. I gave Bobbie some money to give you so ask her to give it to you I love you I gotta go. I hung up the phone. Bobbie went into the room and came back and gave me the money. So it was forty bucks and I brought some weed and smoke with bobby. Then we left on the way terry started laughing what you laughing at you know you the luckiest guy in the world.what you mean you just got paid for some shit I know you did and you know you did. We were walking up the street and saw Dwayne coming down the other way. Hey yall what's up man I know you didn't do it and thanks for finding out who did it. The police told us and here's a little something for finding out who did it. Thanks he gave me 20 dollars and we left. When we got in the house terry started laughing to hard. Whats wrong with you man. I can't believe they just paid you fro breaking into their house. I wouldn't have believed it but I saw it with my own eyes. Man that's one to grow on we high fived each other and rolled up our weed and got high. Before we knew it Bruce was home and we had to tell him what kind of day we having. We told him about Bobbie and Dwayne and the chicks. He just laughed and said the sun shines on a dog ass nigga sometimes and theirs nothing you can do about it. So we asked him was he going over the girl's house with us. What I'm going for so when yall get ready to get it on again I'll have to leave again. No thanks but I got me a pussy date and I'm not going to pass it up. We understand so we kicked it with him until it was time to go. Bruce men are you going to get the car yeah why do yall want me to drop yall off before I leave. Yeah what time is you going to get sunny's car. I already got the car. Well what we sitting here for. Because I don't have much money and there's no gas in the car. Didn't we tell you that June and Dwayne just paid this fool for breaking in their house. How much you gonna give me. How much you need. How much are you going to give me? Would twenty dollars be enough? Thanks man let's go what are we sitting here for. We put on our shit and we left we got in the car and went to the gas station and then drove around lil while we went up to skate city to see who was hanging out but no one was outside so we kept going. We went by Pam's house but she was at the skating rink so we went to pick up Bruce's date plus it was getting close to going over the girl's house Bruce's date lived on 87th street so about time we went to pick her up and came back on the low end it will be time to go over the girls house we got to Bruce's date house fast plus I want to see what she looked like and terry did to cause Bruce be telling us how he keep the baldest chicks but he don't bring them by the house so we really had to see what this girl look like. We pulled up in front of her house and Bruce went to ring the door bell I told terry if she looks fucked up when we get home I'm going to let him have it he came back to the car and terry told him what I said I told you that she wasn't one of his best but she was cool she came out the house and locked the door and turned around she looked good ass hell and Bruce said she was all right well Bruce if she is alright give me you alright and you can't take my so fine yeah cuz she looks good let her get up here so I got out the front seat and got in the back and we were on our way to the girls house. Bruce introduced her to us. These are my lil cousins the one behind me is terry how are you doing the one behind you is Bryon or sly dog how are you doing, what do you like to be called Bryon or sly dog which ever one you like I'll call you sly dog cause that sounds cool how old are you 14 and terry how old are you 18 hey I got a sister your age terry yeah maybe one day we can all go out some time I think she'll like you. Well hook it up how about me I got a lil cousin for you she's about your age 14, 13 or 15 something like that there going out with us hell no just us they got their own dates ya'll got your own dates. How I'm going to hook you up with my sister and lil cousin all these girls are just friends or I'll see what you're talking about. that's cool when we pull up in front of the girls house they were on the porch and ran to the car Liz gave Bruce a fucked up look like who? The fuck is this bitch. Hey Bruce hey ya'll. Well here you are Liz asked Bruce was he going to come in and he said no he was going on a date all this is your date he said yeah her name is Tracy and this is Liz and Linda and the lil girl on the porch is their sister Dee. Alright see ya'll later she asked if she could use the bathroom before they left and they said yes. Liz told me to show her where the bathroom was and I did she asked me why did that lil girl give me that fucked up look oh you seen that, yeah I seen that. What she got a thing for Bruce man that lil girl better go sit her ass down some where Bruce is a grown ass man and she's a lil ass girl. Fuck them big titties, she still a lil ass girl. Which one are you here to see the one you're talking about. Yeah, I'm going to hook you up with my lil cousin because that lil bitch, she's on some nothing. Let me use the bath room and I'll be right out then she closed the door I went back on the porch and she was right Liz was all up in Bruce's face asking him about her? Like all that's your girl. I just look and went back in the house. then she came out the bathroom. do Bruce have your number yeah we live in the same house that's cool I got your number. Then I'll call you tomorrow when I get up wit my lil cousin, because that lil bitch isn't for you. Okay look at her? All in his face alright sly dog I'll call you tomorrow okay ya'll have a nice time. Bruce sees you later at the house all he not coming home tonight you'll see him tomorrow. Take it lite ya'll and then they drove off and we went in the house Liz had this mad look on her face and I asked her what was wrong she said nothing and we went in the house upstairs to Liz room cause that's the place we always kick it and started rolling up the weed she kept that look on her face and terry asked me what was wrong with her I told him I didn't know and her lil sister Dee told me she was mad that Bruce left and I took Dee in the other room to ask her why was she mad she told me that Liz had liked Bruce and she was going to break up with me so she could talk to Bruce cause he was older and he had a car. So now she pissed off I told Dee to go in her room and went back in the room everybody was in. Liz asked me where did you go to put Dee to bed and use the bathroom, terry and Linda had all ready rolled up the weed and Liz told Linda to go get the drinks so we're smoking and waiting for

Linda to bring our drinks and the bell rong. We did go to the door to see who it was but we looked out the window it was two other guys Linda came upstairs to get Liz to tell her the door was for her and she went down stairs to the door and Linda stayed up stairs with us I went down stairs to see what was going on but I didn't go in the front room where they could see me I just went in the kitchen so I could hear them talk. What's up Liz you told us to come over here well here we are I told you to come at 7:00 now it's 9:00 we can't have nobody in the house and my mother's on her way home so you got to go before she pulls up and thinks you were in my house. that's cool how about tomorrow yeah come about 7:00 and don't be late hold on tell Linda come to the door before we leave all right I'll be back I ran back upstairs before she could see me she came in the room and told Linda to come here and I told terry what was going on and we both ran to the kitchen so we could here what they were talking about the dude asked Linda could he come over tomorrow she said yeah and they closed the door we ran back upstairs and acted like we never left the room they came back in the room like nothing happened let me hit that joint. Terry gave Linda the joint and asked her who was at the door Linda looked at Liz some dudes that Liz know I don't know them I asked Liz who are they nobody don't even trip they gone I didn't say nothing but terry went into a thing do you think I am some stupid muther fucker or something. If you didn't know who it was you wouldn't asked him to come over here tomorrow I'm not hereing that terry I'm not thinking about that lil boy I got me a man and that's what I want a man not some boy and she took him in her room to talk to him so I went off on liz and she looked at me like I was crazy don't' try to pull that bull shit on me. I'm not her lil dumb ass I don't want to here that. This is my house, and I can have who? Ever I want to come here. So as you can see it wasn't working so I flipped the script yeah like Bruce who? you heard me like Bruce I'm not on that yes you are that's why you were mad when you see that girl in the car like you were his woman no I wasn't mad about that I was mad because Linda had on my shoes yeah right? Think what you, want to. why would I try to go with your cousin and you live in the same house how do that look let just chill out and kick it and she gave me another drink and kissed me and we got down to business this time her pussy wasn't that big and it wasn't that small but it was smaller then last time. Terry knocked on the door I was like tarry im not finish and I told him I'll be right out I went in the bathroom to wash up and terry came in there I'm not going to be fucking with this girl anymore and I told her that she started crying and went to sleep how are you going to tell that girl you're not going to fuckwith her anymore and then fuck her it was our last fuck so whats up with you and liz were cool man I think your crazy so I knocked on liz door to tell her to come lock their door and we went home the next day me and terry went over pam house to see her and tammie tammie was there but pam was gone with pickles I asked tammie was pam kicking it with pickles again and she said yeah, so I knew it wasn't no getting back up with her so I asked terry how long was it going to be before we went back home he said a lil while and I asked tammie could I use her phone and she said yeah so I called liz and asked her was it cool to come over there and she said yeah and asked me to bring terry I told her that terry and linda had broke up she said she knew that's why she wanted me to bring him over there so she could get them back together I told her I would try and she said do what you can cause this girl is over here acting crazy like she is going to do something to herself and I don't want that to happen so I told terry what was up and he said he'll think about it all the time he knew he was going over there cause tammie was acting like she didn't want to give him any pussy anymore. She was playing hard to get plus she have's a new boyfriend and you know how it goes when they get them a new man all the pussy you used to get is over with plus that's their mans pussy now. So he was in the room tring to get her to up the pussy and I'm waiting in the other room like a flunkie just looking at TV the phone rung and tammin said it was for me I got it and it was Liz. You not at home where are you? Over some friends house it better not be some girl it's just some people who we grew up with are you still coming over here yeah after we leave from here alright don't forget to brine terry with you okay I got you later. terry was getting mad cause she kept playing with the pussy so I knew terry was going to go over liz house with me cause he wanted some pussy we left tammie house and went back to the crib and tammie called our house to tell me that that girl called for you again and I told her you went home she should be calling I told her thank you, but she would hang up. I aske her if she wanted to talk to terry but said said no and kept talking to me like who is that girl what did I do to her is she sprung what do she look like where did I meet" er at I just went on and told her I had to get off the phon so that she could call she told me to call her back after I got off the phone with her and I told her I would but I was lying and soon as I hung up the phone it rang and it was liz. Hello may I speak to bryon yeah it's me I thought you were going to come over here after you left you friends housed I was but we stopped home first are you still coming over here yeap let me talk to terry I yelled down stairs to tell terry to get the phone and went in the bathroom but bruce thought I said the phone was for him and he picked it up when I came out the bathroom bruce was on the phone nigga the phone is not for you. it was for terry she's talking to me so sweet I thought it was for me terry phone and terry come to the phone and it was liz on the phone she asked terry was he going to still come over there and he said yeah then she asked him was bruce still there and he said yeah she said put bruce back on the phone and he did bruce told terry to go get me and terry came and got me and bruce pointed at the phone and told me to listen she was talking all about how she wanted to get up with him but I was all in the way and that girl he was with was not good looking he should get up with her and he said what about bryon and she said what about him if you said you'll get up with me I'll drop his ass so fast his head will fall off just come over here tonight and don't bring his ass and you'll see bruce said okay and she said don't forget to bring terry and hung up the phone. I asked Bruce what was he going to do he looked at me and his eye's lit up I'm going over there not without me. you know they don't want you there just me and terry do me like I did you when you were over there and you wanted to fuck her I left so you could get the pussy and I'm just asked for you to do the same I know you're not going to be a cock blocker no I'm not on that go do your thang so terry and bruce left to go over there girls house I called over there but I gave them time to get over there the first time I called liz picked up the phone and I asked were they over there and she said no but I can hear them in the back ground so I told her that I was waiting for them to comeback so I could come over there and she said cool and hung up the phone the next time I called over there linda picked up the phone and I asked her was they over there and she said no and I told her I was waiting for them to come back so we could come over there and I asked to talk to liz and she came to the phone are you still coming over yeah soon as they get back she said ok and hung up the phone the last time I called linda picked up the phone and I asked to speak to liz and she said liz went to bed I knew what was going on

So I didn't call back anymore, but then the phone ran and I thought it was Liz or one of them but it wasn't, it was Tammie, so I talked to her for a while until I got sleepy. When they came in the house I asked Bruce what happened, "we fucked" and my heart was broke at 14 it was my first time that I knew how cold hearted a woman could be. I didn't cry I just went in the basement and got in the bed and went to sleep. The next morning I got up and asked Terry what really went down I knew what had happened but I just wanted to hear it from terry. He told me they got fucked up then Liz put them out her room and ran to the bathroom to take a shower and walked back in her room ass hole naked and Bruce fucked her brains out. I could here her calling his name from the other room and Linda told him that Liz and I would never have worked out because Liz liked grown ass men. She used to fuck our play uncle, this guy who used to go with our mother his brother when she was only 13 and he was 24 ever since then she'll talk to boy's but she'll only fucked grown men she said cause they got big dicks and she don't have a lil girls pussy any more when he told me that I couldn't do nothing but look. and felt my heart, fall to my feet. but I still wanted to be with her cause she needs someone her own age to be her boyfriend and not some grown ass man her mother's age so I called her and asked her if she wanted me to come over tonight and she said I'll think about it, okay cause you was supposed to come over her last night but didn't. so I got to think about all right cool I'll call you later then I went in the basement and asked bruce was he going to make liz his girlfriend. He looked at me, "you like this girl don't you", and I said yeah. let me tell you, you were right about she got a big pussy you were right that girl don't be fucking no lil boys she got a womans pussy for show cause I had to do to her what I do to the vets and I'm not talking about girls my age I'm talking abut the women 28, 29 and 30's them ages she was cool but I don't want her for a girlfriend? And you shouldn't either. But you got to find out, for yourself. But I'm not going to fuck her anymore so you don't have to worry, about that. go ahead make her your girlfriend. but I'm telling you not to do it okay, okay love you man but know it's on you not me to put up with the bull shit like all them other nigga's she is going to have. you can't make a hoe your girlfriend. but you're going to find that out on your own you're young and you got a lot to learn but I'm telling you this one right. Know I didn't care what Bruce was talking about cause I wanted to be with her and I felt that she needed to be with someone her own age to kick it with and talk to so all that day I stayed in the house and waited for her to call back but she didn't. and night began to fall so I called her can I speak to liz this is liz whats up who is this it's me, me who you know who can I come over I haven't made up my mind if I want to see you call me back in an hour. okay I'll call you back in a hour. An hour went past and I called her back she was acting like she didn't want to see me so that made me real mad so I went outside to cool off and I seen my man Prarie what's up nigga what are you doing nothing do you want to go over these chic's house with me he said okay, so I went back in the house to call Liz and see if she want me to come over I called her and she was still acting like she was crazy so I knew I had to go over there even if she said no I told prarie to wait for me and not to go any where cause these chic's were hot and I need someone to come kick it with me he waited for me and I went back in the house to call Liz for the last time before I went over there I called and asked to speak to liz. She got on the phone and went into a thang what in the hell do you keep calling for, I don't want to see you where is Bruce I don't' want you anymore and don't call back and she hung up the phone. Now I'm on some I don't give a fuck if she don't want to see me she is going to see me anyway !I told prarie come on and we walked around her house I ranged the door bell and nobody came to the door I rung the door bell again and still nobody came so I knocked on the window and nobody came to the window so I pushed on the window and it came open and I climbed in and opened the door for prarie and he came in and we went upstairs soon as they seen us liz went into a thing what the fuck are you doing in my house what the fuck you think I'm doing in your house I came here to kick your ass, boy get the fuck out and I hit her in her eye and she fell to the floor and I kept hitting her, her sister Linda tried to help her but I knocked her down to and kicked her in her back prarie just stood there and looked at me like I just lost my mind and didn't do anything I didn't give a fuck because in my mind I was doing the right thing for me and her she need me to do this to help her get on the right track I told her I love her even if she fucked my cousin but she was so scared that I was going to kill her she just layed on the floor and so did linda her lil sister dee came running in the room and I knocked her down and picked up a can of raid and put some fire to it and told her if she didn't stay down I was going to light her up and she was too scared to move what prarie was on takening all of these people shit while I'm on some love sick nigga shit he's stealing what he can get and I'm not paying it any mind cause I'm out of my mind for this girl so I just pull myself together and just left her house and went home the next day it was like I didn't do a thing I just went to school and came home like I didn't do anything but everybody knew what I did and gave me that look like your'e the crazy lil nigga we know but I didn't let it go to my head I just kept it cool and acted like I was on nothing after school I just went in the house and did what I was supposed to do at home like my home work and take out the trash but the police came and got my ass right after the talk bobby and sunny had with me the next day before sonny and bobby sat me down to tell me to slow my ass down. Bobby knew me real good and he knew my mother and father so he know what I was going through but sunny wasn't there to talk he was there to kick my ass and let me know I was still a lil boy but for some reason he gave me a pass but told me the next time I fuck up it was my ass. I was glad I didn't get my ass kicked but the next day I wish I did I was on my way home from school and it was a police care in front of my house I didn't think nothing about it then the police man asked me what was my name and I told him and he put me in the car then another car pulled up with liz and linda in it they jumped out the car yeah that's him and the police said are you sure yeah I'm sure that's that ass hole and they took me away to the police station when I got there they took me upstairs and put me in a room by myself and asked me where is the other guy that was with you I don't know what your talking about you don't know what I'm talking about wait here next think you know they brought prarie in the room you don't know him no he's the one told us where you dumb ass live but you don't know him alright. It's cool we got you ass now they took me in another room where everybody was liz was in there her sisters linda and dee plus their mother and father and prarie I knew it wasn't looking good for me as dee told the story to the police it made me look too dangerous to be on the street and they made it look like I made prarie took their shit and he went right along with it.to make me the fall guy I put him up to it and if he didn't do it I was going to kill him and it was nothing I could do to help myself but just sit there and keep my mough closed cause if I open it I would get in deeper shit then I was in so I just smiled and laughed until the police lady said she'll beat the shit out of me if I keep laughing and I stop doing that quick I knew I was in a lof of trouble but I just didn't know how much, after she took their statement they left even prarie I thought they would let me go after a lil while but that didn't happen they took my dumb ass to the audy home and I stayed in there for three months before they sent me to D.O.C st. charles where I learned a whole new way of life. I had been in the audy home before but I had never bee to D.O.C. it was my first time going I heard lots of stories about it but I've never been there before when we came through the gates it looked like I knew I was in a whole new world the place was so big and all you could see was this big ass gates around the whole place the van pulled up to intake and we got out and went inside the intake and they put our shit on the floor and told us to sit down they took the cuffs off us and told us to have a seat. We sat down and looked around the place it was me and 8 other guys I could look in their face and tell that 5 of the guys were scared to death. This young guy came from around the back he looked around our age I said to myself he can't be working here but he was brought our jump suits out to put on and I asked was he a staff member he just laughed and told me no I'm in jail just like you but you have on your own clothes. I'm a cross the streets whats across the street. I'm in st. Charles you cats just in intake so if we go across the street we can wear our own clothes. Yeah then he pulled out a pack of smokes. What you can smoke across the street yeah you can smoke can we smoke yeah then I asked for one and he gave me one. I was trying to hide it but he told me I didn't have to do that. So I smoked it in the open and the staff didn't say anything. The rest of the guys were looking at me like I was crazy but this one guy he was white he asked me to save him some and I did he asked me have I ever been in here before and I told him no. he said he had and told me how the place was ran, we would be in intake for about 2 months and then they would decide where they would put us if we would go across the street or if we would go to another camp like dupage or Warrenville. We changed our shit and they gave us our paper to tell us what cottage we were going to it was owens and robinon or kennedy king at the time our cottage were going to the dinning room to eat dinner so they took us to the dinning room to meet up with our college. I went to king cottage and two other guys every body else went to owens and robinson when we got to the dinning room I was looking around it looked like some shit off tv about jail then it hit me I was in jail for real no women just niggas and some female staff but mostly niggas I can't lie I got a lil scared but I didn't let them nigga know that then we got to the second floor of the dinning room who did I see across the room Richard who used to go with my cousin bobbie and I just smiled and he looked at me and laughed and then smiled to whats up boy you finally made it down here. Bobby told me you were locked up just getting here yeah don't worry I got you I got the whole st. charles for the folks if you have any problems just tell me cool I know you need some smokes I'll have some for you tomorrow when we come to breakfast alright cool, cool and I didn't give a fuck anymore about anybody fucking with me we went back to cottage we had about two hours before we went to bed and this dude came up to me and asked me what I was and I asked him do he know Richard and he said yeah I told him to ask him what I was I don't have to ask him I'm asking you then the staff came out and told us it was time to go to bed so I went in my room I knew the next day I might have to kick this nigga's ass if he got in my face so I did some push ups and was getting myself ready for this cat just in case he tried some shit the next morning on our way to breakfast he came over there where I was and asked me again man who are you to ask me what I am you don't call nothing here my cousin Richard call it for kennedy and king and he's across the street we'll if he tell me to tell you what I am I'll tell you we got up to the dinning room and Richard was at the door soon as we came in I told him about this nigga sweating me and he told dude I was folks but I wasn't I had been to some of the folks meetings but I was just a lil disciple at the time and didn't really become folks and Richard came over and gave me four packs of cigs then dude came over to my table so you're folks what did he tell you he told me that's cool my name is Kevin and I gave him five and we sat down to eat he pointed out the rest of the folks to me then we got through eating and went back to the cottage when we got back he was still on my back asking me all types of shit where was I from who I used to hang with where did we party and I just got tired of listening to him and told him to get out my face and let me have a peace of mind he didn't like that he told me don't you know I could get you a (v) for talking to me like that and I told him let me tell you something don't you know I can get your spot if you keep talking to me like that so he went on about his business and left me alone so I just sat there and watched tv and the other folks came over there to introduce their selves to me I met the guys but what was all in my head if these niggas find out I'm not one of them they are going to try to fuck me up I need to get cool with some of these guys so I went in my room and got a pack of smokes and gave all the folks one and the brothers but I didn't give any nutron shit and made jokes about them what could they do jump me people and folks would woop their asses then it was time to go to bed and I went in my room and thought about what I did, I knew I was wrong cause I wasn't nothing but a nutron myself who got hooked up buy some body who knew me on the streets so the next day I came out before we went to breakfast I gave all the nutrons a smoke and nobody else and the whole cottage just looked when we go to the dinning room Richard was at the door again with more smokes for me and some goodies and he told me to work in the kitchen the next day so he could hook me up with some shit when they come from commasay so I ask the staff if I could work in the kitchen tomorrow and they told me to sign up and I did the next day I was in the kitchen working on the front line Richard had the hook up and I was glad to be his boy my two months of intake went by so fast before you knew it, it was time for me to go across the street and I want to go to Richard's cottage but Richard was going home in the next two weeks so I went to cleven cottage with one of the guys who I knew through intake I didn't make that much money intake working in the kitchen but it gave me a chance to meet a lot of the others guys from these other cottages that were all ready across the street plus I got to see Richard more before he left he told me he was going to leave me his tv and radio when he leaves in two weeks I was so happy for him but I wish it was me cause all in my mind was when he left these niggas was going to try me but I was ready for them I had my own room, but nothing is in it that's why I was hoping that Richard left me the tv and radio cause if he did that I would even come out of my room the two weeks went by fast and the day before he was leaving he came to the dinning room and told me that he couldn't get the staff to bring the tv and radio to me so I told him don't trip if he can just get me some clothes it was this staff name mr daniels who was really cool he bought the clothes over to me I ask if he could bring the radio and tv he said blake asked me the same thing but I cant do that clothes are onthing tv and radios are another I told him thank you and gave him five and went to the office so that they could put my name on my clothes I need clothes more then I need that tv and radio cause I only had two pairs of pants and three shirts and all of them were state clothes but the clothes I came in with Richard gave me two pair of jeans and nine shirts boy was I happy cause I didn't have anybody to send me clothes my mother and father were deceased and I had no others family who gave a fuck about me and the people I was living with had no money to send me I was shit out of luck if it wasn't for Richard in st. charles with me I wouldn't have shit at all and being across the street and wearing state clothes in st charles is a no no they would ride your ass like a horse it was the last day that I would see Richard and he said he had something for me before he left. Richard told me to meet him in the bathroom, I went in and he came in after me he had something in his hand inside some tissue he opened it up and I was like that's not what I think it is, hell yeah it's weed man be cool before you get us fucked up and he gave it to me at that time I haven't seen weed in 7 months boy I couldn't wait to get some where I could smoke it plus he let me know if I got caught with it that was three months added on to my time so I had to play it cool and get rid of it quick to so I found somebody I could smoke it with and we went outside the dinning room for a smoke break a weed smoke break this guy named micheal was cool with me so I asked him if he wanted to smoke some weed with me and he said cool we lit it up and began smoking then Kevin came out side and ask what we were doing can't you see we're getting our smoke on where did you get some weed from, my cousin who is leaving today I didn't like Kevin that much cause he was always acting like he was the shit or something and I couldn't stand that. My buzz was just kicking in when this asshole had to say some crazy Shit. That's not weed? what the fuck are you talking about man that's sage that stuff we get in the kitchen man get the fuck out of here I got this weed from my cousin Richard who's going home today let me see it I had a little left that I didn't roll up and I showed it to him he went back in the dinning room and came back out with some stuff that look like weed but it didn't smell like weed so we knew we had some weed and he just looked stupid don't you feel like an ass he was madder then a mutha fucker I could see it in his face as he went back in the dinning room by this time the weed had kicked in and I was feeling good as hell next thing you know out comes angie, angie was the staff who ran the kitchen at st charels she was a lil white woman with big hips but no ass and she was not that old she was about 27 or 28 and kind of cold in her own way but what I like about her she wasn't prejudice and she didn't take no shit but her teeth looked like she ate shit besides that angie was cool she came outside the dinning room to see what we were doing whats going on out here we were just taking a smoke break whats that I smell micheal I lit some leaves on fire and we put it out don't be out here starting no fire and hurry up and get back to work okay we will be there in a minute and she went back in the dinning room I lit up the last joint that we had rolled and began smoking it then micheal came back out side to aske me why I told angie that he was out here lighting leaves on fire I couldn't tell her we were out her smoking weed why didn't you tell her you were out here lighting leaves cause she would have told me to come back in the dinning room and we wouldn't be smoking this joint right now, good point next time you get the blame okay I can deal with that and we went back in the dinning room to finish our work we had to clean out the pots and pans to get ready for our dinner food and clean up the kitchen for the next shift that was coming on after us, at this time you could go back to the cottage cause I couldn't smoke it there so I stayed so I could smoke the rest of my weed the dinner shift came in and we got ready to prepare the dinner food I need a new side kick to smoke weed with cause micheal had went back to the cotage so I got this new guy from intake to smoke with me his name was paul Watson he just got to st charles and he was kind of scared cause it was his first time there I told him it was my first time too and just don't let nobody punk him out and he'll be cool after we prepared dinner I asked the staff if we could go outside for a smoke brake and they said yeah so me and paul went outside I fired up a smoke and then I fired up a join the looked at me like I was crazy you smoke weed in here hell no but I think you need this to cool you down he took a hit of the joint and smiled man that's some good weed where did you get it I got it from my cousin he went home today can you get some more, yeah it's no problem when you across the streets you just have to have money not the money on the books the real money that you can put in your hand I can get some money on my next visit well soon as you can get the money I can get the weed we smoked two joints and then we went back to work he told me he was going to get a visit tomorrow could I get him some weed by thin I told him yeah know I couldn't get no weed but I thought he couldn't get no money but the next day he did he had 20 bucks and asked me how much weed could he get and I told him about one bag he gave me the money at breakfast and I todl him I'll have the weed by lunch not knowing where I was going to get some weed from I took his money cause I haven't seen money in about 8 months I almost forgot what it looked like so I had to have it then I thought about I can give this dude some sage he's a white boy he don't know any better so I hooked him up some sage and put it in some paper lunch time came around I gave it to him with a smile I was across the street and he was in intake what could he do to me and plus he was a white boy all he could do was tell the staff so I wasn't worried about him kicking my ass just telling on me but what could they do but take the money back from me I thought about going back to the cottage after serving lunch but I said fuck it I'm going to stay till dinner room close so we got ready to serve dinner I had about a haf a joint left so I went outside to smoke it by myself and think I'm outside the dinning room all by myself in the gangway smoking a joint even thought I'm not free it was the close thinking to it cause all that time in the audy home we were never outside to smell clean air with that lil smell of weed in the air made me feel free even though I wasn't after while Appleton called me in to go back to work he was the dinning room evening shift staff a big fat black man who talks a lot of shit Appleton was alright but he all ways would work the shit out of them kids from intake cause he knew they would come to the dinning room to work just to get out of their cottage in intake you did get that much out of the room time cause it wasn't like across the street intake went like this go to breakfast back in the room go to dinner do the count come out for four or five hours back in the room until the next day, that's why I was glad that I was across the street we had more freedom we were almost done with dinner food so Appleton told all of us that were across the street to take a break and gave us some smokes he was like that if you didn't have smokes he'll give you a pack but when you made store you had to give him two packs of smokes back it was cool but a lot of the kids in intake never made store cause they would owe Appleton soon as it would be time for them to turn in their time sheets they would have to turn them over to Appleton cause they owe him everything I never had that problem with him he liked me for some reason or another cause if I got a pack of smokes from him I never had to pay him two back I just had to pay him one back so one day I asked him why did he like me like that because I reminded him of his son that died he said I look a lil like him and acted just like him. He had got killed in a car crash when he was about my age plus he thought I was that bad of a kid cause he read my fail and knew about my mother and father's death and said that's what made me do the things that got me put in st charles and he was right I didn't act a ass until they passed I didn't have a reason. So me and Appleton bonded that day and kick it tell it was time to serve dinner I had never been on the front line before close as I got to that was passing out milk but this day Appleton put me on the front line and on the front line in the dinning room means you got pull in st charles the first cottage came through nigga's looking at me, like chief hook me up know you're going to hook up your folks so I look out for them a brother I knew came through the line I knew had juice for the lords and the stones just knew I was going to do him wrong and give him a lil bit of food I look him in his eye and gave him much food as I could he smiled and said thank you G, and in this place you don't hear words like that coming from some body not in the same mob as you so I was feeling real good about myself we went through cottage so fast before you knew it intake came up andI had for got about dude next thing you know he was in my face hook me up you know I got the muches me to hook your boy up to man I'm to high I got the munchies I could do nothing but laugh he asked me to get him some more weed okay I'll have it for you tomorrow and went on about his business and I laughed my ass off everybody thought I was going crazy, but me. Since Richard had left I've had to make a name for myself. I had 18 months to do and I wasn't going to be nobody's punk, plus I had the gift of gab, no one was going to out smart me. The staff or nobody. We finished up the dinner line and made the staks. We just had to past them out to all of the cottages and I liked to do that because everybody in st. Charles knew me because I was the only student who came to every cottage so I could move shit like kits, weed or what ever. Since I didn't have real weed I was moving sage until nigga's got wise to me but I didn't care, I had made hundreds in st. charles and no student but me had money in his pocket and we wasn't allowed to have money I had st. charles on lock. Ten months had gone by and I was getting ready to go to the review board to see if I could get out early. I was playing it cool not getting into shit with the students or the staff because I was getting ready to go home. One year had passed and I had only 6 months to go. I had money on the books from working in the kitchen and I had money in my pocket from working in st. charles I wasn't having any problems to top it off Appleton became cottage manager and put me in his cottage he wasn't working in the dinning room anymore and I couldn't sell anymore fake weed so I quit working in the dinning room the same time. He did and just chilled in the cottage I would do the clean ups in the cottage to get some extra points so when we went to the teen center to play the game I was always on the top five the top five also get to go to the dance when the girls came from warnville to the teen center. I would never forget my first dance I bought clothes from people who were in other cottages who had new clothes and Appleton got me some cologne, I was ready for the chicks plus I haven't seen a chic who wasn't a staff for a whole year, we made it to the teen center on dance night and I was ready. I came in the teen center and the girls wasn't there yet so I went to play pac*man and this nigga came fucking with me, you got to be on the top five to play the pac man, o yeah you got to be on the top 3 to come to the dance so what the fuck are you talking about, hey man I'm just fucking with you I use to be your cousin room mate, who Richard? Yeah Richard and he told me to look out for you but I see I don't have to look out for you; you're looking out for yourself. You only been here a year and you're the man, coming to the dance, the richest nigga in st. Charles I heard about you. You'll be getting out soon, yeah well just be cool and you'll get out sooner then you think, you're on the right track, thanks man. Then I just kept playing the game before you know it the girls had came in and I knew one of them from the world I use to go with the girls sister Deborah and her name was Irma I was like Irma hey! Wait let me sign in she went to sign in and come over where I was at to talk to me she told me her sister Deborah was locked up in Warrenville. She was going to tell her that she saw me and I was looking good and smelling well to. **We kicked it for the rest of the night tell it was time for them to go** back to Warrenville and it was time for us to go back to the cottage on the ride back to the cottage I was feeling to good cause I knew I was going home soon and I would be back with females, while everybody else would be thinking about the next dance when we got back to the cottage it wasn't time go to bed yet for us but I went anyways cause I wanted to make it a good night I didn't want these nigga's in my face asking me how the dance went cause I was going to hear that all day tomorrow so I went to sleep. The next day when I got up just like I thought they was all in my face how was the dance and I would tell them the story it just didn't stop in the cottage it went on in the school in every class how was the dance not just students , but staff too, it was like I was the star of st charles and I just came from a big show everybody who's cottage was going to the dance after that came to me to ask what to do at the dance and I told them. time went by fast after that and before you know it, it's time for me to get out. Since I didn't have a mother or father to come home to they looked for me a group home for me. So it took a lil while for me to get out they found one for me on the west side it was call the Austin group home and thay put me in it, it was a big mansion, on the west side on mason and Washington at the time it was just me there and the sander's who owned the house and their daughter len she looked all right but she was knocked up len was cool like a sister she was around my age so that gave me some on to talk to cause I have been gone for all most two years and I didn't know that much about the west side but I did have people who lived over here but I just didn't know where they lived I stayed in most of the time and watched tv, they had cable and I never seen cable before it had a show with all black people called BET. And I like it the show I like the most was this show called video soul it had all the black people who sang on it like prince, Michael Jackson, and everybody. I had just got there but the Austin group home was alright they took me shopping and enrolled me in school plus I had the money I made in st. Charles. The Austin group home was a big place it had three rooms on one floor and two of the rooms that two beds in it and the real big room had four beds in it but I was the only one there it had a tv room and a pool room in the bastment, plus the house was so big if you didn't live there you could get lost I started school and I had to go down town to school I was at the smith academy it was alright but not a lot of girls and I had been around nigga from 1981-1983 I didn't need to meet anymore nigga's but it was what it was, school and I had to deal with it and they had me going to this after school shit to help me get a job that was on the south side and it gave me a chance to move around a lil bit and I was getting used to the world. I had only been out two weeks and one day I was on my way home from the job training school and this guy came up to me and asked for a light I gave it to him and the train came we got on the train and it took off, two stops later he snatched this women's chain off her neck and jumps off the train the women sits there looking all fucked up and I was feeling bad for her and some body on the trian said one of them is steal back there and I said who me, I didn't know that dude and the train pulled off, someone told the conductor who runs the train that I was with that chain snatcher. The train stopped but the door didn't open we just sat at the station I knew what was coming next. When the door opened in came the police and took my ass to jail for no reason I just knew I wasn't going back to jail for this cause I had nothing to do with it but the police looked at my record and seen I just got out of st. charles and my ass was out, locked back up in the audy home and on my way back to st. charles for some shit I know I didn't do but they didn't want to hear that I was on the first bus smoking back to st. charles I couldn't believe it I seen people get out and was back in two months or three saying they didn't do shit and I was like yeah right but I seen this shit first hand and couldn't believe it I had just got out of here two weeks ago and I'm right back in here for some shit I didn't do I was mad ass hell. Now I got to start over for nothing when I got to intake I knew the routine so that didn't bother me what really bothered me was the shit I was going to have to hear from the nigga's who knew me from across the street. Hey you back I knew you ass was coming right back but two weeks you must didn't like the outside world. I knew they were going to let me have it so when the staff asked me if I wanted to work in the kitchen I said yeah the day after I got there the next day I was in the kitchen one of the kitchen staff knew me hey your' that boy who used to work for Appleton do you want to work on the front line, I said yeah, might as well get it over with cause they were going to see me anyway the ront line was not like it was at first when I frist came to st charles now it was front street line as the cottage came through everybody asked me I thought you were going home man, I just looked stupid standing there like a jack ass but what really fucked me up is when my own college came through the dinning room and looked me in the face, I knew what was going through their heads but what really fucked me up was when Appleton seen me I could tell by the look on his face he was disappointed in me like I was his real son and the staff in the kitchen didn't make it any better hey Appleton I got your son back on the front line he just looked at me and put his head down and walke away he didn't even talk to me and I knew he was disappointed in me but couldn't say shit. What was I going to tell him that I got caught up and I had nothing to do with it, he heard that before not form me but a lot of boys like me that night I went back to the cottage and went in my room and cried like a baby and went to sleep the next day I didn't work in the kitchen I just stayed at the cottage and when it was time for lock up one of the staff came to me and gave me two packs of smokes and said they were from Appleton and I was like cool and went in my room. I was feeling a little better cause I didn't have any smokes plus Appleton was the only friend I had in st charles who I knew would look out for me so I put my name on the list for kitchen detail so that I could talk to him tomorrow the next day when they came to get me the staff gave me a funny look like who do you think you are got the staff brining you smokes I didn't give them any lip cause they would beat you ass and send you to lockup to fast and I didn't want any problems I just want to go to the kitchen do some work and talk to Appleton when we got to the dinning room angie was working and she haven't see me and she was like hell no not you again cause she was on vacation when I came back well I don't' got to tell you what to do just come in the kitchen and help me get breakfast started so I went in the kitchen and help angie get breakfast started but I could tell it was a lot of students in intake who didn't like the way a lot of the staff were looking out for me and wanted to start some trouble with me cause one of them accused me of being a trick but that shit stopped when I caught his ass down the wing one day and beat the shit out of him I didn't have that problem anymore but it was other cats trying to get me to hook up with them hey the word across the street is you're folks but you don't' act like you folks you don't sit with us you don't talk to us what up with that. I just do my own thing I knew since Richard had left and he was holding down the whole st charles for the folks and he told thm I was folks even though I wasn't I couldn't tell them I wasn't and everybody said I was then I would have to fight the whole st charles so I kept to my self and hoped that nobody asked me law until I could get back across the street where I didn't have to put up with this bull shit I did three weeks all ready and in two weeks I would be back across the streets and Appleton pulled some strins so that I would be going back to my old cottage in about two weeks I just had to be cool till then but you know shit don't run smooth when you want it to the next week folks want to have a meeting and I had to go to it to see what they were talking about I really went there to see if they were talking about me but they weren't they wanted to know who knew their laws and I knew I didn't know nothing but I acted like I knew everything so they didn't pay me no mind and just went on about their business that week went by and the next week came they wanted to have another meeting this time they wanted me to open up the meeting and I didn't no what to say so I told them I didn't no my laws and they told me they were going to give me two weeks to learn it and I didn't' care cause in two weeks I would be across the streets and there was nothing they could do about it so they gave me their laws on paper and told me to learn them I said okay and paid it no mine I just wanted to get the fuck away from these ass holes and in the next few days it was going to happen I keep my cool like I was learning the laws but never picked up the paper then one day I was in my room with nothing to do and started reading the laws they were kind of cool and before I knew it I had learned them all in one day, after I learned the lit, the dude who gave it to me came to aske me if I learned any of it and for some reason I just didn't like this guy so I told him no just to see what he would say, "you got one week left so you better get on top of it", I laughed and said okay then this other dude came over who I was cool with and ask me if I wanted him to help me with it and I told him I knew it he didn't believe me so I took him to the wing and spit it for him, he couldn't believe it and he asked me why I didn't just tell him I knew it all ready and I told him I just didn't like that guy, he said yeah and I told him I didn't know but I just don't like him he laughed at me and told me I was crazy but I was a cool mutha fucker and he gave me five. Later on that night he came back around to aske me that same shit, not the guy I was cool With.the ass hole. I didn't like! so I told him I knew all of it and he told me to spit it and if I didn't know all of it he was going to hit me in my mouth so we went to the wing at the end of the hall and I spit it for him all of it and he gave me five I'm glad you knew it or I was going to have to hit you in your mouth I siad oh yeah you weren't going to hit me in the mouth, if you didn't know it so I stole on his ass and started beating the shit out of him by this time the guy I was cool with and some of the other folks came down the hall to get me off his ass before the staff came what went wrong didn't you spit it for him, yeah I did, don't you know all of it yeah so why are you fighting, he told me he was going to hit me in the mouth and I don' t like that shit I don't give a fuck who he is and the dude i was cool with walked me off so I knew I was going to have to watch my back cause he didn't like it I pulled his hoe care cause he used to act big and bad till I bet the shit out of him and he came back down to earth. The dude who I was cool with became my friend his name was james and he was from 87th street out south and alright dude his room was across the hall from mine and at night we used to talk about shit we used to do in the world and how we were going to hook up when we get out, two days after the fight I had with dude my paper came for me to go across the street and I was leaving that next day james told me that nigga was going to try to pull it with me before I leave so I was on point when we went to breakfast the next day I kept that nigga in front of me so I could watch him and after breakfast, coming out the dinning room he tried to steal on me but I knew what he was on so I kicked his ass in front of the whole st charles before I left intake and went across the street. I didn't have to go to Roosevelt cause the staff seen him come at me I was in the back of the line and he was in the front so he came all the way to the back of the line to get his ass kicked and I loved it, it gave me more respect and let other mutha fuckers know that I will fight so don't come fucking with me I did what I had to do they took his dumb ass to Roosevelt it was lock up in st. charles when you fuck up and I went back to cottage to pack my stuff to go across the streeet the next day that night me and james kicked it all night till it was time to go to bed and when we went in our rooms we kicked it until it was almost morning I couldn't wait to go across the street, you would think I was going home from the way I was acting, the next morning I got up getting ready to go to the intake to get my stuff so that I could go across the street but they told me it wouldn't be until later on that day so we went to breakfast and then we went to lunch and I was getting inpatient waiting it was getting close to dinner and Roosevelt let that nigga out that I couldn't stand I was just waiting for him to give me a look or anything and I was going to beat the shit out of him but the staff came to me and told me to get my shit I was leaving I was to happy when we made it to the cottage I got out with my stuff and took it to the office they have to check your stuff to make sure you didn't bring what you're not supposed to have in the cottage. As they looked through my things I just sat in the living room watching tv all the rest of the students were in their rooms it was almost time to go to dinner and they just got out of school so there was nobody in the living room but me, after they got through looking through my stuff they took me to my new room it was on. A wing. Room 14 it had bunk beds in it I never had a room mate since I was in ST Charles so I knew this was going to be a new aspect. I put my things away and got ready to go to the dinning room for dinner I heard the door lock pop and it was time to go, we all came out and lined up along side B wing, we walked to the dinning room there was no talking in line all you could hear was the staff calling for a signal 4 to the dinning room a singal 4 is when the staff needs a van to farlow they use at night just in case somebody wanted to run and I didn't see why. you can't get over the fence, plus it's covered with bob wire and it's 15 feet tall and if you get caught that's another 6 months to a year added on to your time, plus I didn't no anybody that made it out I was feeling good walking to the dinning room in my own clothes and not having on that intake shit it made me feel free even though I wasn't when we got to the dinning room I didn't know where to sit so I sat by myself cause everybody sat with their own. Stones would sit with stones, folks would sit with folks and it was this new gang I had never heard of called the vice lords it wasn't a lot of them but they didn't let nobody fuck with them and I liked that we ate and went back to the cottage you have to go to your room when the staff is taking count and then you can come out after they get through when we came out to the day room I just sat by myself and watched tv and waited for someone to say something to me, I met this one dude who would change my whole life but at the time I didn't know that. He came up to me and asked me my name I told him and he told me his name was kenny doss, I didn't know what it was about him I just liked him he asked me what I was and I said I was folks he laugh and said he was a vice lord and I told him I never heard of vice lords till I came to st. charles he told me you must be from out south and I told him yes, me and him kicked it for about an hour until the rest of the students came out their rooms doss took me to the dude who was holding it down for the folks named reggie he took me to the side and asked me to spit some lit and I spit it for him and he introduced me to the rest of the folks. We kicked it for a minute then it was time when one wing was taking a shower the other wing was in the day room when that wing got finish the other wing would go to their rooms so that they could take a shower me and doss were on the same wing and reggie was on the other wing, so when reggie wing went to take a shower me and doss went back to kicking it. He asked me where was I from on the south side I told him 56$^{th}$ street and I asked him have he ever been over there he said no and I asked him where was he from he told me the west side around homan and adams and I asked him was that close to Monroe he told me it was the next block and I told him get the fuck out of here I got a brother who lives over there he said what's his name, curtis what does he look like I don't know I never seen him before my father told me about him before he died but I never met him I bet your brother curtis is big curtis off Monroe his mother runs the snowball stand on Monroe cause I don't know another curtis around there on Monroe, but that one what does he look like, he looks a little like you but he's dark skined and tall, he's one of the brothers one of the brothers what do you mean, he's a vice lord he's a vice lord yeah are there a lot of vice lords on the west side that's all you see man I feel like I'm stupid or something cause I never heard of vice lords before I came to st charles me and doss kicked it until it was time to get ready to take our shower and then we kicked it until it was time to go to bed. The next day when we got up reggie came to me to tell me where to get in line at on our way to the dinning room, we were all in the back of the line and I asked him yeah we were all in the back he told me that was the way it was supposed to be, since the beginning was vice lords and then the stones and then the BGDN when he said that I looked around at all the other cottages and it was all the same but until he told me that I never knew. It was a lot of stuff I didn't know but I was learning as I went along. The next months went by fast and I had been across the street for 5 months already but

I had not gotten a room mate yet, doss and the guy he was in the room with wasn't getting along and he wanted to change room so he asked me would I like to be his room mate, and I said it was cool with me, he went to the staff and asked if he could move in the room with me, the first staff said no you have to ask your cottage manager I told doss don't' trip cause Appleton was our cottage manager, me and doss was cool with Appleton so when Appleton came in to work we asked him and he said yes but he didn't want no shit out of us, we told him we were cool and he said you know what I'm talking about that vice lord/folks shit don't come to me later talking about you can't be in the same room cause one of ya'll is this and the other is that cause I don't' want to hear it Ok! Appleton. and we moved in the same room I was happy doss was in the room with me cause I didn't have a tv or radio and doss and both plus doss kept money on the books and we kept store in our room lots of the time we didn't eve come out to the day room, we would just sit in our room and watch tv until the power would go off then we would talk untild we would go to sleep, I couldn't ask for a better room mate then one day one of the folks asked me to write down the law for him and I did, he was new and because folks in intake and didn't know his laws so I had to write it down for him and doss asked me what was I doing and I told him and he asked me to let him see it and I told him no, then he said. Ill shows you my lit? could I look at yours and I said yes but you know we can both get fucked up for doing this, we laughed and gave each other five and our papers I was reading the vice lors laws and it was not like ours it was more deep like words from the bible it was so deep I asked doss was it's hard to learn it he told me no then he asked me do you know all of this shit and I told him yeah, I think your lying go ahead ask me whats the frist law and I told him whats number 10 and I told him hats number 16 and I told him, whats number 4 and I told him whats number 5 and I told him number 7 I told him hey, look here you can go from 1 to 16 and I know them all now its your turn spt the frist one, what is the frist it's only four on this paper we don't go by number we go by names tell me the name and I'll spit the statement of love and he spit, the holy devine and he spit the lord of lords and he spit it I had to give him props and had to give me mine cause what I had to learn and what he and had to learn was some deep shit just a different way of thinking. So we just kept teaching each other laws to pass the time before you knew it I knew all of his and he knew all of mine but nobody knew that we new it we used to laught at every new cat who came through the door who didn't know their shit no matter what they was, I remember one time this cat came from intake and everyone was at school but me I had a staffing that day that meant you stay at the cottage for a meeting with the staff I asked him what he was and he told me he was a vice lord so I asked him to spit it and he didn't know a think so I went in my room and wrote it down for him and told him be better know it by the time the rest of the brothers come back or he was going to get his ass wooped he better know one by hard and when everybody came back I took him to doss and told him to spit it he learned one by hard and asked him how many of the brothers did he know he said just me and doss laughed at him nigga that nigga aint no vice lords that niggas a disciples that's my room mate and he be on bull shit don't let that nigga get you caught up and he would do the same thing to the new folks that would come through when we both got our new jobs at intake we use to have so much fun fucking with them until one day we were at the cottage playing cards me and doss were kicking ass and taking names we had all ready won three games of spades and was on our fourth win when james started talking shit it was alright at first then he took it to far by calling doss a hook and I checked him, hey man you're out of pocket talking to my room mate like that, man I say what the fuck I wanna say this is my mouth plus you act like you're one of them niggas and not one of us anyways we're not just playing one hook we're playing two after he said that I couldn't do nothing but hit him in his mouth and that kicked it off I hit him his partner hit me doss hit his partner and the whole cottage went up over a card game but what was so funny about the whole thing he was right I didn't feel like them cause all the time in st charles everybody who I got in to it with was folks I had over 15 to 17 firghts and all but all of them was with folks and one was with a stone I never had a fight with any vice lors right then I knew I was going to be a vice lord for life the staff called a 10 10 that's a riot and they locked us down on both wings us on a wing and the folks on b wing while we were locked down on the wings doss looked at me and said welcome home lord you're one of us now and I couldn't do nothing but laugh cause he was right I made it known who I was riding with durning the riot so I commited treezin so that meant I wasn't one of them any more doss said do you want to get blessed in right now and I said might as well I've been fighting all ready two brothers steped up to me and so we fout for about two to five mins and then doss stop the fight and they gave me love then the riot staff came in to take our ass to Roosevelt when we got to Roosevelt I could see james ass and the rest of the niggas we were fighting in the hole cell he yelled out the cell nigga you're off count you might as well be one of them mutha fuckers and I looked at him and said I am and flagged the vs. the staff took us in the back of Roosevelt and made us sit down and asked us what kicked off the riot and I told them we were playing cards and reggie kept talking to me and doss like we were punks and that's what started the riot, Appleton came down to Roosevelt and went off cause it happened when he wasn't there they put us all in our cells, me and doss were put in the same cell so me and doss kicked it for the rest of the night until it was almost morning. The next day when we got up I asked doss more about being a vice lord and he told me all about it, I had already new vice lords law but he taught me about all of the brands it was CVL's, TVL's, RVL's, IVL's, 4CH's, UTVL's and UVL'S, doss was a uvl unknow vice lord he told me all the laws were the same for each branch and ask me what branch was I going to represent, I told him I can't represent nothing but unknown cause unknown showed me nothing but love he showed me how to throw up unknown and who our king was and the don of the nation plus the prince at that time if you would have asked me if I would ever meet these people I would have told you no, doss told me, about when he was on the brickes they were getting a lot of money and kicking it with the badest bitches and how much fun it was around where he lived and how they used to get in to it with the souls and I had to ask him what's a soul and he told me what a soul is it's like folks but their not folks they are under the black diamond and so are the 4CH's but the 4CH's are vice lords and the souls are souls but their first cousin to the 4CH's the more he talked the more I loved being a vice lord it had meaning, it had a reason and it was more like a family plus the name was cool to vice lord second two god and next to jesus you couldn't be no better then that. I had now found a home and doss was one of my brothers for the rest of my life, we kicked it more until it was time to eat breakfast in Roosevelt, you eat in your cell and they bring your food to you. We had got used to being in the cell cause we been there for four days already and was waiting to go to court to see if they were going to ship us out to lil joliet or let us go back to the cottage a week had gone by and we were still waiting, then the staff teen came in for court they took us one by one and made up their minds up what they were going to do with us when doss time came to see the board I knew what ever they was going to do with him they were going to do to me, they came and got him out the cell and took him to the board room he was in there for about 15 or 20 mins and he came back lord they gave me 6 months plus they sending me to lil joliet well I know if they did that to you I got the same thing coming they didn't get me that day I went to court two days later they gave me 6 months plus they were sending me to Lil Joliet to, I didn't care about going toLil Joliet I just really didn't care about the 6 months they were giving me I already had to do 12 months plus with 6 months that makes 18 months. Almost 2 years not telling how much time I might get in Lil Joilet cause I knew it was going to be somebody that's going to try something, and I knew I was going to have to kick their ass. Some of the guys that were in the riot with us went back to the cottage and some was taking that ride with us to Lil Joliet. Bad ass James use to act like he was glad that they didn't send him to Lil Joliet. He took a whole year set time not to go. But he sent a kite about me to the Folks atLil Joliet. By this nigga name Jesse who thought that if he would give them the kite that they wouldn't fuck with him but with me. But I didn't care if I didn't have anybody in the whole prison down here with me as long as one nigga name doss. That's all I needed when we got to Lil Joliet. And we got to intake we could tell they didn't take any shit. They would kick your ass with no problem, and Jesse found that out on day one. By trying to pass that kite a staff member named Big Charles akaBig Chillie. Big Chillie beat the shit out of him for trying to pass that piece of paper about me. Look you stupid mother-fucker you must think I don't know what a kite is who gave your dumb ass this to bring this shit from St Charles. What happned in St Charles stays in St Charles? I would put this size 11 Boot up your ass understand. He looked at the paper and said who the hell Waddell is. I put my hand up. Come here I hope I'm not going to have no trouble out of you. No sir, I liked he called me sir Waddell you just got some cool points. But that nigga there is on my shit list. Hey this nigga tried to pass a kite about you. Do you want to read it? I read it and it says that I was folks and I fliped to Vice Lord and I was helping folks get jumped on. And that I wasn't real folks. So Big Chillie said you read that shit. So I'm going to throw this shit away. But I don't want any trouble out of you. I'm not going to have to kick your ass right. No! Waddell go get your ass back in line. Yes sir I walked back and got back in line. He sent Jesse ass to lock up on the first day. He said dumb ass I'll see your ass in a week ok. Jesse started crying like a bitch. I just looked and started smiling. We had to stay in intake for a week before they told us what dorm we were in. See it was only five dorms and one of them was the school dorm. A week had passed by, and they were handing out what dorm we where going to. I got sent to dorm 5 and doss got sent to dorm 2. We asked if we could be put into the same dorm no was the answer. Their reason was that they didn't want us to start no trouble. So as I was going to my dorm I told doss to keep his head up. He said you be cool. The dorm was different than the cottages in St Charles. The dorm was much bigger and the cells had steel doors. Not like the one's thay had in St. Charles if you kicked them hard enough you'll kick them open. The day room was big ass hell with steel benches. When I finally made it to my dorm it was time for lights out. So I'm laying down wondering what tomorrow may bring. But one thing for sure what ever it brings my way I was going to handle my business. That was in my mind until I fell asleep. When we got up the next morning and went in the day room. Everybody was looking at me because they didn't see me come in last night. Not like in St Charles we had sinks in our cell. But we have a toliet in the cell here and had to go to the day room to wash up. So while I was waiting on a sink to be free a guy came up to me and asked me what I was. I told him I was a vice lord and he looked at me with a funny looked. So I went back to my cell to put up my shit and another guy came up to me and asked the same question. What are you? I told him and he gave me the same look. By this time it's breakfast time so I didn't know nobody. So I got in the front of the line. I knew that's where lords were supposed to be. Everybody look at me with a fucked up look. But I didn't care because if they didn't like it they could bring it. I was letting them know I'm not scared of nothing. So when we got in the dinning room I sat at the first table I seen. Nobody came over to sit with me I didn't care. This other dude was about to sit at this table and the guys told him to go to the table with his kind. So he came over to my table and asked me was I peoples? I said Yeah and he sat down. I'm glad it's finally another brother in here besides me. You mean that we're the only people in here. I just laughed and we gave each other five. He told me his name and I told him my mine. Hey man where you from, man I'm off 53rd yeah I know some people from over there. This cat name jock-o yeah I know that cat, he's off my block where are you from I'm off 56th. What? Is there Vice Lords over there? No, but it will be when I get home. I told him what happened while I was at St Charles, and how I became a Vice Lord. He laughed and said I know you wish you were folks now.

Hell no they didn't care for me so why should I care about them. Plus I found out that my daddy use to be a Vice lord. I got a brother that I haven't never even seen and he's a Vice lord.

What the fuck I look like being folks when Vice lords are in my blood. But when they find out that you was folks they are going to come at you. I don't care I'll get there ass one at a time. Plus I was never real folks anyway my cousin was, he held it down in St Charles. He just told everybody I was so no one would mess with me. When he left they thought they could pull my hoe card. But they couldn't I kicked about fifteen folks asses. But not at one time I kicked their ass and told them I was a Vice lord. That kicked the riot off and that's what got me here. Man, dog you're a motherfucker I'm glad you on my side. If they fight you they fight me. Good to hear I got one nigga on my side I just wish you were on the same wing as me. I asked him how old he was, he was15 just like me, but it seemed like I was his big brother. I knew I had to hold him down. It was time to go breakfast was over. Soon as we got back to the dorms a fight breakout in one of the other wings. At first I could see who was fighting but when they brought them out I see its rashawn he says I'm holding it down dog. I just looked at him and smiled one of the other guys says what the fuck you smiling at. I knew if I let this nigga punk me I was going to be punked the rest of the time I was there for. So I just stole on his ass and started kicking his ass until the rest of his gang jumped in. I didn't care because I had his ass.The staff came and broke it up. I was still smiling they knew it wasn't no punking me. They were going to give me my respect up in dorm five. Staff took us to lockup that's over in intake when I walked in rashawn was too happy to see me. Man I thought you was one of them niggas talking shit. Man my word is my bond and I seen how those niggas tried to come down on you because you were talking to me. I told you I got your back so how in the hell I'm gonna **leave you hanging. Staff asked what started the fight and I said I was** the only Vice lord on my wing. They didn't like it because rashawn was talking to me and got into it with their folks and that I was smiling. Staff says what and went to talk to them about it. They dumb asses said yes. They let me go and locked there dumb asses up. I didn't tell the staff that I stole on them first. When I got back to the dorm everybody was looking at me like how in the hell he got out of that. I sat down at the back of the dayroom with my back against the wall just in case one of these punks try and steal on me. I would see it coming and be ready to fight. Nobody tried nothing I guess they know it's not that sweet. They knew if they tried any thing that I was going to get down with their asses. Plus they thought I was kind of crazy. Because when I got back to the dorm I let them know I didn't give a fuck how many folks it is in this wing don't fuck with me and I want fuck with you. Nobody said anything they just kept on watching TV and laughing. Staff comes in because it's time for school I had just got there so I wasn't in school yet. Everybody had left for school and I just sat in the dayroom thinking could it get any worst. Just as I thought, that. In walk this dude the same nigga that tried to bring a kite in about me. Jesse pussy ass. He was one of them folks for protection ass niggas. But I didn't care I was already into it with them niggas. As soon as he saw me he tried to talk to me saying man I don't have anything against you I was just doing what they told me to. Feel me man, hell nah and don't say shit else to me or we will be fighting like I said. Jesse was on of them niggas riding the nation for protection niggas. He didn't say shit else he just sat his ass down. He's kind of scared of me because he knew I didn't like his ass. Not because of what he did but because he was one of does niggas that never fought for his self but got the folks to do it for him. Because he knew he couldn't fight. We just sat there and watched TV until it was time for lunch.When everybody came back you could tell Jesse ass was scared. He didn't know who was who and what was what. He was trying his best to hang around me like we were cool. But I kept moving around making his ass look stupid. Before you knew it was time to line up for lunch so I go to the front of the line like I always do. This nigga jumps right behind me so I didn't say anything. Soon as we get in the dinning room and I get my tray and go sit at my table. Here comes this nigga and try to sit at my table I just said fuck it nigga why in the fuck are you all under me. See dude over there he's one of your folks go sit with him. Hey gee dog here's one of your folks on the new. Jesse got up from my table and went and sat at the other table. I sat at the table and ate by myself I got use to it. Plus I didn't trust these niggas up in here no ways. Two weeks had passed and I was use to being the only nigga under the VL on dorm five. Then three of the folks went home and three brothers came to the dorm. I couldn't believe it they came right when we got out of school. One of the folks told them how I was and they came over to me. Whats up lord we be people they told me their names one of them was named Eric and the other was Daniel and David. Two of the brother's came from out west and one was from up north. Eric and Daniel were from out west and David up north. Eric and Daniel was cvl's and daivd was a cvl. So they asked me how many other brothers were on the dorm, and I said you looking at him. How long have you been here I told them 3 months and 2 weeks and you were the only brother here? Yeah and they didn't fuck with me. They tried too but got what they were looking for a good ass kicking. I didn't care how many motherfuckers it was I fought all them. They weren't going to punk me. Man lord you got a lot of heart. No I had to do what I had to do well we will finish kicking it after dinner. A Few minutes later it was time to line up for dinner so I do what I always do go get in the front of the line. All the other brothers were in the back of the line. I told the entire brothers to come to the front of the line with me. The folks didn't like that but what they really didn't like was we were getting deep on deck. Even though it was just four of us it seemed like it was 20. All the time they had been there it had not been any brothers on dorm 5. I had been there for three months and it had only been one brother on another dorm and he had been there for two years. I was the first brother he had seen on dorm 5 in a long time. We didn't care how deep the folks were we just wanted to do our time to get back in the world. We were all kids in a kids jail acting like we were in a summer camp for boys but it was jail. A lot of these guys were going to the big time after they turned 21. Time was flying by since some of the brothers got here I had someone to play spades with talk to and eat with. I could relax and do my time and not let time do me. A lot of the folks were going home and a lot of white boys kept coming in. And before you knew it there were only three folks and still we weren't triping off that all we wanted to do was our time and get the fuck out of Lil Joliet. I had already done a year and had six months more to do, and if I had any good time I would be going home in three months. On Fridays we had goals to make sure the brothers were in line we weren't on nothing but getting out of here. We would go to school and I would kick it with doss he had got some good time and would be going home soon. I was really happy for him he had already done three years before we kicked off that riot in St Charles. He had about two months to go before we did that shit had happened. Before we knew it a riot broke out in dorm 2 and doss was in dorm 2 I hope his dumb ass wasn't in it. The next day when we got to school I was looking for doss ass. But his ass came in late he came in and I told him I thought you were in that riot. Hell no my ass want to go home fuck that shit I'm to close to getting out of here. I can't fuck up now but you are going to trip out it was folks. What the fuck they fighting each other for. Because there are no more BGDn they broke that shit up and now its only Bd's and God's and BG's. Everybody got their own king and their own chiefs. That way their fighting some of their own. Some of them ride under David and some under Hoover and some under Boonies black. Their making their play for who is going to run the joint for the folks. Man I know you were tripping out on that shit. I already knew what was going down my mans told me that some dude brought a kite in from the big Joliet for the folks. Saying if a niggard ant God folks kick their ass. Doss man how deep is this most of them naggers flipped God, but some bd. Well that ant got nothing to do with us. Before we could sit down the school had went up all you could hear in the hallways was God bad killer's naggers beating the shit out of each other. All the brothers run in the room where we at and just watched the shit go down. I tell you I've seen it for myself the birth of GD nation. Them naggers came through and did there thing. Some of them tried to run in the room where we was but we didn't have shit to do with that. We did let one of doss friends come in there he was one of them. But we didn't let them come in and fuck with him we told them he was one of us. The staff came and took all them naggers and it was so funny, because a lot of them cats didn't want to flip there flag. I couldn't stand them naggers remember I told you that dorm 5 only had 4 brothers. After that shit happened most of dorm 5 was peoples. It was too funny to me because most of them cats that tried to get me in trouble were now calling me chief. I could say I didn't like it but the shit went on for four or five months before it calmed down. After it calmed down ill Joliet had more brothers than folks in it. Everybody that said they were folks was God's now. It wasn't a bad or big in the whole Lil Joliet, and if somebody came in on the new and said they were folks they had to be a god or those naggers would run them naggers out. I and doss was holding it down for the brothers. All the naggers that wanted to be a vice lord had to be unknowns or they wasn't going to be shit. That's the way me and doss wanted it most of the joint was unknown vice lords, and next in to us in numbers were the GD'S and next were stones. The stones were holding down ill Joliet until I got there. Doss went home before me I had six months to do after he got out. I told him that when I got out I would hook up with him. But that never happened a month after he got home he got killed by the souls in a war with the unknowns that was my niggard. My six months has passed and I was back on the bricks. They sent me back to the Austin group home on the Westside. I was glad to be there because I was not alone it were some other cats in the house. Now it was this cat name Joe Sanders and this dude name Lawrence. Joe sander was an ill ass bitch niggard, but Lawrence was a cool dude. That's why I made Lawrence my roommate. We kicked it everywhere together we went to parties down town. We had to sleep on the train after the parties. Because it would be too late to get in the house we had to wait to the next day. It was cool until they told me I was moving to a group home in Chicago Heights. I sure was pissed off. I just got off parole and had a job as a messenger downtown. Now I had to find me something else in the evening. They put me out in the suburbs, I hated it but the only good thing came out of it was I found my cousin Tommie. He had a car and on the weekends he would come and pick me up and bring me to the city. He would pick me up on the weekends and we would kick it all weekend. I and Tommie were real close. Tommie use to come to my house all the time when he was little. When his mother aunt Ruth would come see my dad and her daughter June. Tommie and I use to talk all the time before my mom and dad died. Tommie was the only one who treated me like family and I loved him for that. But back to the store one day before I left the Austin group home. One day Tommie and one of his partners came to the door and asked for Lynn. I open the door and didn't pay them any attention and called for Lynn, but on my way back upstairs Tommie called me by name. I looked and saw that it was Tommie and said whets up cut. Long time don't see so I asked Mr. Sanders could I have company because I haven't seen my cousin in a long time. He said yes so we went in the basement to play pool and get caught up on things until it was time for him to go. He gave me his number and told me that he would tell aunt Ruth he seen me and that we would kick it next weekend. When the next weekend came I had already moved to Chicago Heights. He picked me up at 95 street and we kicked it at aunt Ruth house. Aunt Ruth had one rule for me I could spend the weekend but I had to go to church on Sundays.

Church was cool though Aunt Ruth was the pastor and I had two cousins that were preachers. Most of the whole church was my family. Most people go to church to find husbands and wave not me because the whole church was my family. If that was the case bobby would have been fucked long time ago. Tommie would take me back to the train station after church on Sundays and I would go back home. He found out how to get to the heights and would come and pick me up on the weekends. I lived in the heights almost a year and they never seen me hang out. I went to prairie state for school and the group home would give us money to spend. So on the weekend I would get my money and go to the Westside of Chicago doing my own thing. I would hang with my cousin Tommie and go to church on Sundays. He lived on arthington and Lawndale right by a school. I would never forget the day I met the brother around there. One day I was in front of the building waiting for Tommie to come home from work I had got out of school and came to the city. I didn't wait for Tommie to come and get me it was about five o clock. There were some guys playing ball in the school yard. So I went over there to play ball with them. It was about six of them playing 21 so I asked could I play. They said cool most of the guys were my ages 17 and a couple were 16 so it was cool. Until this one kid name Donnie started going off about his call and started some shit. He hit this one boy in the eye and his brother tried to help him he hit him too. He left and said he'll be back he went on Polk street to his house. He came back with his brother's red-dog and Craig. This was the first time I would meet people like me. They came on the court who's fucking with my brother and nobody said shit. They asked this one guy what he was and he said nothing and they hit him in his shit. They asked me what I was I'm an unknown vice lord what are you. Red looked at me hey man I'm an unknown vice lord too. Then he gave me love. We been the best of friends every since and never had problem. My cousin Tommie pulls up and get out the car. Hey red that's my cousin. Hey Tommie this is your cousin he's alright he's one of us. Tommie looked at me and said you're a vice lord. Yeah man, from around here, yeah you know them no that are some crazy shit. I thought they were trying to kick your ass. They were until they found out that I was an unknown like them. We just got in the car and rode around until it was time to go in the house. The next day when Tommie went to work I went on Polk Street to kick it with the brothers. First person I see when I get on Polk was Donnie. I went up to him and told him who I was and we kicked it until Tommie got off work. When Tommie came around on Polk he introduced me to the rest of the brothers. We left and drove around the hood looking for girls. We didn't run into any chics. We just got tired of riding and went in the house. Tommie didn't have to work that day so I rode with him to his dad's house. Uncle Tommie lived in an old folk's home downtown in a real nice building. When we got their Uncle Tommie came down to bring ill Tommie some money. I see you got your buddy with you. Hey Uncle Tommie how you doing. I'm doing fine you better not get my boy in no trouble. Uncle Tommie I don't get in trouble no more I'm a good boy. Yeah right and he walked away and went back upstairs. Me and Tommie left and went to go dip on these girls that we met early. Tommie girl was a dark skinned girl and the one that I was digging was light skinned. But for some reason Tommie liked the one that I liked. So I told him when we get there tell the light skinned one to get in the front with you. So when we got there the girl that liked me started to get in the back. Tommie says get up here with me. No imp cool I want to be back here with him. Tommie was a little pissed off but I didn't say anything. So we drove to get something to eat Tommie was trying to act like big Willie. We get to the restraint and he orders his food tell the girls to order there's he asks me what I wanted. I told him he thought I didn't have any money. But I didn't say nothing Aunt Ruth gave me money this morning she knew I didn't have anything so she gave me 50 dollars. So we told the waitress wanted we wanted he pulls his money out and says you could've been with me but you wanted to be with him. You could have been down with a man with money but you wanted to be with a broke man. She look him in the face and said imp not a money hungry bitch I'm a good looking bitch who like good looking naggers. I got my own money freak. That really pissed him off. Then she told him he was too old for her anyway. So he got mad and didn't want to pay for her food. So I paid for it he really got mad then. When we got back in the car he asked us where we were going. Man whets wrong with you. Nothing I and my girl wanted to be together. So I told him to let us out at the bus stop. We got on the bus and went downtown and had a good time on 20 bucks. When it was time to leave we got on the bus I took her home. She says you can pick me up anytime you like. Tommie was parked outside their house when we got back. The girl he was with was mad than a motherfucker because they didn't do shit. And she had to be stuck in the house. I got in the car with his ass. So what's all that shit was about? You know I wanted to be with her ass. Hell it's not fault you tried money and even your car but she still wanted to be with me. I told your ass to try and get her and if she chose you I would get with the other one. Man you don't have to worry about me no more when I get my ass home that's where imp staying. So after this weekend I want be going back with his ass. When I got home and start to make plans for the next weekend I thought about my step brothers who had been trying to get me to come and go to parties with them. Tommie called me on Thursday I told him that I was staying home and I would call him when I was coming back out west. The weekend had come and I was on charge at school doing what I do. I couldn't wait to go kick it but this day was not the same I could feel it. Plus this chick kept checking me out so when it was time to go in the teen center I asked her you must like me. What would make you think a thing like that? Because you have been watching me all day or I must be going crazy. No you not going crazy my friend is the one who likes you. Who just as I said who her friend came in the teen center. I introduced my self and look at her. She was a skinny girl but it was cool. She told me her name was Paula. I asked her had she had lunch yet. No so would you like to have lunch with me. So we went to the lunch room and grab something to eat sat down and started to talk. She told me all about her and I told her about me. She was a pre law student that wanted to be a lawyer and that was cool with me. I was a business law student and she had one class with me. She was like a friend to me instead of a girlfriend we had become real cool with each other. She uses to pick me up for school and drop me off. We didn't get into each other until we had been around each other for a while. Then one day it just happened we started kissing and it was on from there. We had not had sex yet but just kissing. One day she just up and said it was over I asked her why and she said I have to get my self together. One day coming home I saw her in the car with this other guy. I called her up and asked her was that her new man. She said yes and that was cool with me. Can't say I wasn't hurt or nothing because I was but I got over it. Went on about my business started meeting people in Chicagoheights by going to parties out there. A lot of people knew I could sing and would give me the mic at the parties. It was around the 80's when prince was doing his thang. So when I would get the mic I would sing prince songs. I liked that a lot so when they weren't playing mix songs I would get the mic and sing it got me a lot of girls and numbers. But then I met this real cool dude at one of the parties he was a DJ his name was markey. He could dance real good to we became real good friends. Markey put me up on a whole new kind of music house music. That was the music that everybody wanted to hear and dance to. Markey showed me how to dress house and dance house. We got in all the parties free it was fun being with him he showed me a whole new thing about the clubs. He put me up on all the right clubs and all the right chics. Plus he knew everbody in the heights. `And University Park. It was the hang out where all the chic's hung around the best looking chic's so I hung out with markey all the time. Markey had this one friend named vick he was a DJ too but didn't have the stuff to DJ with. But markey was cool like that to let him use his DJ stuff and he would make money too. We would go with him to some of the clubs while he DJ we would get all the drinks we wanted for free anything we wanted. Plus vick had some of the finest sisters in University Park a nigga had ever seen. And at every party vick thought he was the shit. My foster brother started tripping on me so I just stopped going to the city and started kicking it harder in the heights. Plus people started knowing who I was. I liked that a lot because I was put on markey's crew.and we were important to the heights. We called ourselves house nation. It was me markey vick Marvin the hat man helton. He got that name because his hair cut was like a hat and that was some funny shit. But don't get me wrong this nigga had lots of women that were crazy ass hell about his ass. My man Jessie was a Mexican that was our five man crew. The south surburbs was our when it came to throwing parties. We had it on locked from country club hill to University Park it belongs to the house nation. There were other crews but they were closer to the city. But they couldn't fuck with us. They would call us to do parties in there part of town but they wouldn't come to our side of town because no one wanted them they call on are crew. They knew we had the badest DJ's that not on the radio. Plus they knew that their party would jump all night long. We had a bad dance crew too and we had our own theme song to house nation. Now who could fuck with that in the 80's around the Chicago area. That's why we had it on locked then Marvin put these chic's in the crew. The next thing we know it was a house nation record by one of the best DJ's Farley jack master funk. You couldn't tell us shit we knew we were the one making shit happen. We inspired Farley to make that song. We made a name for our self and were making good money doing it. This was far from the shit I was use to doing gang banging, stealing and breaking in people's house. I like doing what I was doing instead of getting in trouble. I didn't want to go back to jail. I'm 17 now and they could put my ass under the jail couldn't get away with the shit I use to do when I was a shorty. Time had flew by a year had passed and I haven't been to the city. Tommie was calling every weekend trying to get me to come to the city to kick it with them. I kept saying no but he thought I was still mad at him. I told him I'm cool out here I'm having fun. So he came out to the heights with me to see what was going on. I took him to one of our parties, he thought it was crazy but he liked the girls and he told me he would be back next weekend. But he didn't come back I just kept on having fun with my foster brother and my new friends. It was the summer of 85 and we had this pool party in Park Forest and it was jumping too hard. By this time marky had showed me how to DJ and I was on the wheels of steel, then Jessie came to get me. There was someone at the door for you I went to the door and it was Tommy I told them to let him in he came in and looked around and looked at all the females in the place in their swim suites and lost his mind. I see why you don't want to come the city anymore, damn it's a lot of fine females in here yeah it's what I do. I went back to the wheels of steel because I had an hour left to DJ before marky got on the table. Tommy wanted me to come kick it with him but I knew I wasn't going anywhere I had just hooked up with this girl named Katie, she looked just like a young Anita baker, plus she was too thick there was no way in the world I was going with this nigga and leave this goddess. I told him to stick around, he said he wanted to but he had some people in the car and I told him to bring them in too, so he went back to the car to get them. He had Joey with him and stacey plus one of my foster brother's mikes, I knew mike wasn't going anywhere plus he had got in free. He had wanted me to get him a ride up here anyways but he used Tommy to do it, it was cool although mike didn't waste any time getting at the females, he broke out to fast while Tommy kept trying to get me to go back to the city. I told him that I couldn't leave until marky came to take my place on the wheels of steel, Joey used to go to my aunts church she was nice looking she was too thick, that's who Tommy was with and he tried to hook me up with stacey she was alright but she didn't have shit on Katie, I'm telling you stacey had some big tittis and no ass and an alright face. Katie had a fine ass face and big tittis, and a round butt. Did I tell you looked like a young Anita Baker and I'm aint lying? E.p.m.d knew what the fuck they were talking about when they made that song for real. When Tommy seen her he was like damn, and I was like hell yeah, so I get them in the party and I went back to the wheels of steel and I had an hour left to go and I was ready to kick it with Katie, stacey came over there by the DJ booth to talk to me, I didn't know you knew how to do this, yeah I've been doing it for a little while now it's cool and it's alright money and keeps me out of trouble and I like it. Then Katie came over to see what we were talking about. Hey what's going on, nothing stacey is an old friend from my aunt's church and she didn't know that I DJ yeah my baby is a good DJ then gave me a kiss and walked off. Stacey looked like that's your girlfriend and I said yeah she smiled and walked off. After a little while Tommy came back to the DJ booth and asked me how long I was going to be, I told him as soon as Markey gets back but I wasn't going back to the city with him but I was going to show him how to get back to my house and he can find his way from there, he said cool but we still had to wait for Markey to come. And Markey finally came, I told him that I had to break out but I would be back before the party was over, he said cool then we went to get in Tommy's car; it was me, Tommy, Joey, stacey and Katie. Stacey and Joey thought I was going back to the city with them but when we pulled up in front of my house they were looking too crazy and said oh you're not going back to the city with us. No we have something to do, I gave Tommy some money for gas and a little for his pocket. I went in the house to see where Mrs. Gray was so I could sneak Katie in the house. She was in the kitchen like always so I snuck Katie in the basement where my room was so that we could do our thing before Mrs. Gray locked the door. She would lock the door at 12 o clocks and it was 10 now. So I had 2 hours to do what I had to do before she locked the door. I told Katie to take her clothes off she looked at me like I was crazy I told her that if we didn't do it now it was going to be a long time before we had the chance to do it again so she was with it. We got right to business, didn't waste any time. Just as we was finishing mike came knocking on the door. Who is it, it's me mike. Hold up I'll be right there, Katie put on her cloths and I opened the door. Mike was like damn, you got big balls bringing her in here. What do you mean this is my room too. No I don't mean it like that, just brining her in the house period. You got balls mallden be tricking yeah you right, hey mike what time is it. It's almost 12, come on Katie let me get you out of here before they lock the door, so mike went upstairs so he could block Mrs. gray and I could sneak Katie out the house, the plan worked good but now I had to get her home so I walked down to marky's house to get her a ride, we lived in beacon hills, and Katie lived in east heights. So I paid marky's brother Kay to take Katie home. It all worked out but one thing, when I got back I couldn't get in the house. So I spent the night at marky's until the next day. Then I went home and when I got there, Mrs. Gray was like how do you like sleeping outside, I didn't sleep outside I went over one of my friends house and spent the night. Yeah right, you spent the night in the back of the house but what she didn't know that wasn't me that was my other foster brother David sleeping in the back of the house. But I didn't tell her that I just let her think that. I went on about my business and I washed up and went back upstairs to call Katie to see what she was doing and to tell her I had a good time and when can I see her again. She told me that her and her friends where coming over Marvin's house to kick it, Marvin lived around the corner from me. I told her that I would get up with her when she came over there, so I put on my clothes and went around there. When I got there Marvin's brother boo opened the door and asked me was I coming to the party later. I didn't know it was a party tonight, he told me that his mother was going out of town for the weekend and Marvin was throwing a party, no wonder Katie and them were coming over they were coming for the party. So I asked boo where was Marvin at and he told me that Marvin was in the room, so I went to the back of the house and when he opened the door it fucked me up, he had all the DJ shit in his room, hey man why didn't you tell me you where having a party, it's for one of the guys who had ranked in the GD's in east heights. And it was his little brother that Kay took the gun from he wasn't supposed to have it he stole it out the house and dude need his gun back, I told Steve I'll see what I can do to get it back and he said cool, I told him to meet me at the party tonight, so we left to meet at Lincoln mall, to pass out flyers for the party we were having tonight. But most of the people in the mall were at the party from the night before. I made them a promise that it wouldn't be any problems and we would party all night long. Plus a lot of the people that come to the party had love for us and knew that we wouldn't let bull shit go down, out of the 40 party's that we had this is the first one where there was a problem they knew that we wouldn't put their lives in danger. After we got finish passing out flyers we went back to Marvin's house to clean up for the party. I told Markey to go get Kay so I could talk to him about giving dude the gun back. Markey pulled me in the other room and told me I had a way of talking to people and getting them to listen to me. He said I had the gift of gab, and I need to use that to make house nation one of the biggest party crews there ever was. And I told him I would do my best. And he put me to the test if you can get Kay to give back that gun you can do anything. Plus you will be the house nation new MC. What's an MC? When we play records you get the Mic and talk to keep the party going and let them know whose spinning and who's on the Mic. Oh okay, I can do that just get Kay over here so I can get him to give that gun back, Markey left to go get Kay, I went home to lay out my clothes for the party, then the bell rang and it was Markey and Kay, I told them to come in and we went into the basement to talk, I took Kay in my room and told him he need to give that gun back, and he said yea because that dude that you took the gun from had rank in east heights. And we don't know how many people got shot with that gun and we don't need to be caught with it. Kay looked at me, you are right but I'm not giving it back to him, you can give it back to him. And I said cool then marky knocked on the door what's up everything cool Kay, yeah he is going to give the gun back, know I said you are going to give it back. And we laughed and then left, I walked Kay and marky to the door and they left went back to Marvin's room to finish laying my cloths out for the party then my foster brother Dave came to tell me the phone for me and I went to the phone and it was my cousin Tommy asking was I coming to the city, I told him no but if he wanted he could come to the heights cause I had another party to do. He said he would think about it but I knew he wasn't coming so we hung up the phone and went back to what I was doing. Then my brother mike came in the house with two of his partners, asking me if I was still going to throw the party I told him yeah, mike said he heard what happened at the party the night before. They wished they could have been there because they didn't like those nigga's from east heights because they always started shit at parties anyways. But they said they would be there to have my back and I was cool with that. I told mike that he and his friends wouldn't have to pay just doesn't let anybody start shit and it would be cool. They left and I called around to Marvin's house to see if they cleaned up already. They told me yes cause it was getting close to party time, but I didn't want to put on my cloths and then have to clean up I told Marvin, I went to get in the shower and put my cloths on and I'll be right over and if mike and his guys come through to let them in. he said bet and we hung up. I hung the phone up and started to get in the shower and then went to put on my clothes then the phone rang for me again and it was Marvin saying that you need to get around here it's already a lot of people but I didn't let them in. I let your guy mike in and told the ones I didn't let in that it was your party and I don't know who to let in. I said cool and hung up the phone and put the rest of my cloths on and walked around the corner. It was about 75 people out there I was like damn this party is going to be the bomb; they were all calling my name like I was some big star "Priest". Let's get this party started and I open the door. All the ladies get in free guys 5 bucks nobody tripped. It wasn't anything but 8:00 and it was already packed. I just knew this party was going to be off the hook. Marvin was spinning on the wheels of steel. The house nation chic's was doing their thing on the dance floor. The only thing I was worried about was Kay and them got here before them nigga's from east heights get here. Just as I was thinking that Kay and Markey and the gang was walking in the door. I was so happy Kay took me in the other room and gave me the gun. I put the gun up in Marvin's room. He told me not to worry he had two guns on him already and Steve said he had two. I took them into Marvin's mom's room to talk to them. I told them to leave the guns in the room until these nigga's show up. Everybody put the guns up Kay pulled me to the side and said hey priest

I love you like you're my lil brother. But I want you to do one thing for me take the bullets out the gun before you give the gun back to them nigga's. Right man they would've shot me with the gun. Much love and I gave him a hug. He said you feel me hell yeah and I took the bullets out the gun and went back to the party. Three hours had past and the east heights nigga's hadn't showed up yet and it was 12:00 so I told Kay if the nigga's don't come tomorrow we selling they shit. We laughed and gave each other five. We were in the kitchen and someone knocked on the back door it was Steve. Hey priest does nigga's from east heights is at the front door asking for you. I told him to put our guys on point. Kay went out the back to the side of the house. Steve went out the front door with me it was a big tall dark skinned nigga. You priest he said I said yeah he said could get that I said yeah wait out here. You would think that I was scared but it didn't faze me. So I walked the nigga to his car and gave it to him. He said man you just saved my life and gave me 20 dollars. He was so happy he kept saying thank you folks. I told him I'm not folks I'm a vice lord. He said thank you brother. Then he got in his car he had about two nigga's in the car with him. And one of the guys with him was his brothers who Kay took the gun from. Hey that's not the dude who took the gun. His brother hit his ass upside the head and told him to be the fuck quiet. And thanked me one more time and they drove off. Out of nowhere came Kay and Stevey when you walked off we hit the bushes we wasn't going to let them get you by that car and let you have it. Even though I didn't see you I knew you were there. We went back in the party mike and his guys were still in the same spot looking out the window when we came through the door we looked at them and started laughing and they started laughing too. They thought we were laughing at the east heights nigga's but we were really laughing at them. We put the guns up and started back having fun. This was one of house nation's best parties we partied until 6:00 in the morning. We cleaned up Marvin's mom house because she was going to be backing that evening. I got done and went home Mrs. Gray was already fussing at mike and soon as I walk through the door she got on me. Where have you been you just like the rest of them don't want to listen to nobody? I just smiled at her and told her I love you mama. And went downstairs to go to sleep. Mrs. Gray was a good lady with a big heart she really loved her foster kids like they were her own. I can't lie we gave her a lots of trouble sometimes. Today is Sunday and I'm not going to church and that made her really mad at me. She played about lots of things but when it came to church she didn't play. So when I finally came up stairs she really let me have it. So I tried to laugh it off but after awhile she really began to make me mad. She knew my aunt Ruth was a preacher and she started to talk bad about her. And she knew I didn't play that and I almost cursed at her. And I thought about who I was talking to and held my tongue. I knew I had to leave out of the house so I went back outside. She comes to the back door and tells me if I couldn't abide by her rules I could find somewhere else to live. I told her that I would do that and went back to Marvin's house so I could cool off. I sat at Marvin's house until his mom came and told me it was time to leave. I walked back around to my house but the door was locked I knocked and she told me that I didn't live there anymore. So I went to Markey house to crash for the night I told him what had happened he let me spend the night. The next morning I went back to the house and Mrs. Gray was already gone to work but Mr. Gray let me in and told me to work it out with her. I didn't even go to school I just sat in the house to wait on her. When she got home she told me that I had to leave. Tried to talk to her but it didn't work so I called my aunt to ask her could I stay and she said it was alright she would have Tommie to come and get me when he got off. He didn't get off until 5 o clock so I had enough time to tell everybody I was leaving. I first went to Marvin's house to let him know. Plus his aunt lived around my aunt so I knew I would see him. Went around to Markey house and he was upset I told him I would be back to do the parties with him. Got back to the house to wait on Tommie and the phone rang it was Katie. She said you weren't going to tell me you were leaving. I told her I was going to tell her but I wasn't leaving her I was just leaving Mrs. Gray's house. I told her she was still my lady and I was going to be coming to see her like always. But I was moving with my aunt in the city so I gave her my aunt's number so you can call anytime you want to. While I was still on the phone with Katie the other end clicked it was Tommie calling me from work he was to happy I was coming to live with them. He told me that he would be leaving work early to pick me up. I told him cool and clicked back over to Katie. That was my cousin telling me that he would be on his way in a little bit. Katie asked me was I going to come by and see her before I leave I said yes and hung up. I went back to finish packing before you knew it Tommie was knocking on the door. When I got to the door Tommie was standing there with a big smile on his face. Come on cuz let's get moving before rush hour. Hey cuz could I go by my girl house before we leave. Yeah man I said okay got my things and said goodbye to everybody and left. We stopped by Katie's she opened the door and gave me a big kiss and said I'm going to miss you. You're not going to miss me because I'll be back next weekend to see you. I told her not to worry nothing was going to change then we left. Tommie was so happy he let me drive back to the city. When we got back to the city the first person I saw was Donnie. Hey what's up Donnie? Hey what's up priest what's been going on with you? Nothing 'what you hanging out at you aunt's for the weekend. No I'm living with them for a little while. Hey man you want to play ball later. That's cool Tommie asks me was I cool then he told me that he didn't like Donnie that much but him and red dog was cool. He uses to go to school with red dog and Craig. We pulled up in the front of their building and it was a lot of kids were in front of the building because it was the summer time. The females were all around the building too. This girl name Betty was out there I knew her from my aunt's church and she was really cool she was about my age and she looked alright. Tommie told me that she uses to like him but he didn't like her. I said what was wrong with her she was to black for him. I didn't get that she was alright to me. So I spoke to her before we went into the building and she smiled and said hello. We went upstairs into the house and aunt Ruth was sitting there hey come give your auntie a kiss. I went and gave her a kiss I said thank you for having me and she said you welcome. I didn't have my own room I had to share a room with Tommie but that was cool. I didn't have my own room at Mrs. Gray's house either. So I put my clothes away and washed up for dinner. Dic came in that was my aunt's husband she married him after she left Tommie's daddy she had been with uncle dic for over 15 years. So Tommie was cool with that. Dic said you made it I'm glad now you can make Tommie stop acting crazy. What you mean, when you stop coming on the weekends Tommie stopped going outside when he would get off work he would just sit in the house and look crazy. I knew he missed hanging out with you. He was so depressed when you stop coming. Look at him he can't wait to go outside. Come on man and get through eating so we can go. Look Ruth I told you he missed his partner he's happy now. Hey Tommie I'll be on the back porch Tommie walked out on the porch. Hey uncle Dic are you for real. Yeah man look at him now. So me and Tommie was on the back porch and I asked him did he really miss me, and he said yeah man you like my brother and I love you. I knew it was my fault that you were mad at me for that shit I pulled with does girls can you forgive me. Don't sweat it cuz I wasn't worried about that. We went and got in the car and drove to Tommie's dad's house to get some money. But when we got there uncle Tommie was outside he started laughing. What's so funny he said you two he looked at Tommie and said I told you he'll be back? I know you did hey dad can I get some money until I get paid. Uncle Tommie looked at me and said you want some money to. I smiled and he handed me 10 bucks, and I was like thank you uncle Tommie, he said don't worry about it now, you two get out of here and don't get in any trouble. Okay see you uncle Tommy, see you dad, love you I love you too and we got in the car and headed back to the Westside. We drove down Chicago ave and made a right on Pulaski and drove down to division and made a left, I asked Tommy where he was going; he said to my brother's house, I said which one and he said Michael. Michael live over here, yeah him and Brenda sanders, I didn't know that they lived on division and keystone. They lived in a big co way building, at this time a lot of purtrican's living around there at this time, and I knew they were Latin kings so I didn't really trip because they were under the Fin, when we got out the car it was a lot of them in front of the building and Tommy was like don't say nothing to these dudes because they might want to gang bang when we walk into the building. One of them said what's up folks and I looked at him and said no folks here we people, he smiled and gave me five he said where ya'll from, Hartington and Lawndale, what type of lord are you. Unknown, that's too cool were unknown kings too. He gave me some love and I gave him some back. Then we went into the building that Michael lived in he lived on the 3$^{rd}$ floor and on our way up it was a whole lot of them mother fuckers in the hallway on our way up the dude I was talking hollowing up the stairs they cool they people. So it was all love they didn't mess with us when we got to the door of Michael's house the door was already open. It was a couple of guys in there with Michael in there kicking, it he told them who we were this is my little brother Tommy and my cousin Bryon but they call him priest. They said what and then they left. Michael closed the door man you missed it was about to go down in here, what happened, you know I been working over here but I didn't know what he was talking about. He was talking to Tommy, so I just sat and listened, man the kings came and shut me down. They thought I was folks and I called Willie and them Tommy it was about50 to 60 nigga's over here to fast the kings seen chief and was like we know who you are. We just didn't know these were some of your people. They called the guy that called it for all the kings around, and we just got all that shit straight see that guy who just left he was the one who call it for the kings he told me don't worry about anybody fucking with me they got my back and if I have any problems to call him and he gave me his number boy Tommy you should have seen how many of them was over here it's still a lot of them in the hallway. It is? Then Michael went to the door and looked down the stairs they were still there and then he made a phone call less than 10 min it was a knock on the back door who is it, chief he open the door and ten brothers came in, one of them took Michael in the room and closed the door they were in there for a lil while and then they came out and left back out Michael locked the back door and came back in the front room where we were at and told us to come in he had two big ass shot guns one was a pump and one was a double shot gun he said dude left them dude's in the hallway to watch your back just in case the police come but just in case they were on something else he left me these guns then it was a knock at the door, who is it give me two, Michael opened the door and gave him something I don't know what it was but after that the dude left and we went back to talking what are you doing Michael? Getting money are you selling drug's what do you think! Man Michael auntie Ruth don't want you doing that shit. Bryon shut up do you want to make some money yeah but not like that not like what you know see that shit. Ok this is what you do Tommy do you want to work hell yeah take this pack if anybody come to the door give them how many they want and get the money, priest you hold this gun and if somebody tries to start some trouble you know what to do okay I'm going to bed. Hey Michael how much money are you going to pay us, Bryon I'll give you 50 and Tommy you'll ET 100. Is that cool it's cool with me how about you it's cool then he went in the room with Brenda sanders and closed the door it was about 12:00 o clock when we started so Tommy called home to tell auntie Ruth that we were spending the night at Michael's house and she said okay all that night people kept coming to the door I couldn't believe it all the way up to 6:00 am in the morning we didn't get no sleep and even though they just kept coming till Michael got up and took over me and Tommy went to sleep and got back up about 5:00 pm that evening Michael asked us did we want to work later on that night I told him no but Tommy said he will be back Michael gave us our money and we left I had 60 bucks and Tommy had 120 and we had nothing to do but kick it

Tommy didn't have to go to work and I was out of school so we went back to auntie Ruth house and changed clothes she told me that my girl Kathy was calling all last night looking for me and she had just called before we came in so I called her back what's up girl you been looking for me, yeah where have you been, over my cousin house we spent the night there last night when are you coming to see me cause I miss you I'll be out there today to come and see you do you want to go to the show that's cool but I don't' have any money don't worry about it I got you I'll talk to you later then hung up the phone. Hey Tommy do you want to go to the show yeah that something to do. I just told my girls we'll be out there hey call her back and tell her bring a friend for me, I called her back and told her to bring a friend for Tommy she said that's cool cause she was going to bring her cousin anyway but her cousin had her own money so I told her we would be to get them about 6:30 and to be ready she said cool then I hung up the phone. Auntie Ruth asked me was the girl I calling around here I told her no then she said was she around where I you used to live and I told her yes then she told me not to call out there cause that was long distance but it was okay for her to call me and I said cool Tommy had just got dressed and I was already dressed so I asked auntie Ruth could I call this last time to tell them we were on our way and she said yes let this be your last time calling out there on this phone and I said yes mame and then I called Kathy she picked up the phone I was just going to call you, porsha want to go. Yes if it's ok. Does she have her own money? You know Porsche always have money. Well we on our way make sure everybody else is there so we don't have to go pick anybody else up ok see you in a minute we hung up the phone. We went to go get in the car and on our way to the car Suzette was coming up the stairs with her two lil boys. Suzette was a fine looking black lady who kept herself looking good her kids too. She had two kids one was about 5 and one was 11 years old. Me and Suzette was cool she was like my god sister. My auntie was a pastor and she didn't let anyone play worldly music in the house so I use to go over to Suzette's house to listen to music. Suzette knew aunt Ruth didn't play that because she was a real preacher and not a fake. Everybody respected her for that. Suzette tells me that she got this new record and wanted to know if I wanted to listen. She knew I liked prince music and she had just bought his new record. Yeah but maybe a little bit later I and Tommie were going to the show. Is that okay with you? Yeah that's fine we left and went to get in the car. We got on the I-290 so we can go to east heights to pick up the girls. While we were on the way Tommy asked me about Suzette. Why you be over her house what you be doing. I just am listening to music. You mean to tell me that you don't be trying to get you some. Let me tell you Suzette is like a big sister to me. When I didn't have anyone to talk too I could talk to her. Suzette takes her time to talk to me because she know I been going through a lot. I love and respect her for that. So looks if you don't have anything good to say about her please don't say it around me. Yo man I didn't mean to make you mad man. No man I didn't mean to go off on you but nigga's is pissing me off when it comes to Suzette. Soon as she walks pass some of them nigga's they are like I wish I could hit that. I let them know that is my god sister and don't be coming like that at her. Let me tell you what happened one day me and red dog and some more nigga's standing outside the building and this one dude kept saying crazy shit about her. I told him not to be talking like that around me. He knew I was pissed off so he said man what did I do to you. He kept right along saying the shit he was saying and red dog told him to cool out. I just stole on the nigga and start whooping his ass. That's why I and Donnie are real cool because he helped me whoop that nigga's ass. And another reason me and Donnie are so cool is because we the same kind of nigga if you don't fuck with us we want fuck with you. So anyway how this girl look that we are going to the show with. It's not one girl fool its two other girls going too. Man get the fuck out of here you mean I get to choose which I want. Man that why I missed your ass from doing shit like this. Well cuz have fun while you can I know you going to like this one girl she's light skinned and she's fine. Cuz you know how I get down when it come to the females. You know I do have good taste. Cuz where do we get off at? Lincoln Highway. When you get to Lincoln highway then head east to Racine and make a right at university then it's the third house on the block. Drive right into the driveway we pulled in the driveway and honked the horn. Katie look out the window and ran out with both arms open gave me a kiss and hug. Tommie got out the car to see what the other girls looked like. Porcha came out and I introduced them. Porscha this is my cousin Tommy Tommy this is porcha they shook hands and said hi. Katie's other friend came out the house and Katie introduced us ya'll this is Annie. Everybody said hello Annie this is my boyfriend Priest and his cousin Tommy. Annie said where you all from are. Tommy answered and said were from the Westside of the city. I have a cousin live on the Southside. Let's get out of here we all got in the car and Porsha jumped in the front seat and we got in the back. Porcha said I know you feel real good. Why you say that. Because you got two fine girls with you on a date. Tommy looked at her and smiled. Porscha asked me how I liked living in the city I told her it was cool the only thing I didn't like was being so far away from my baby. They all just said ooh and laugh. Hey Priest how we get to the show. I told him we were going to Park Forest and Porscha showed him the rest of way. When we got there we had about 10 or 15 minutes before the movie starts. So we kicked it in the car until it started. Annie asked me a lot of questions because porscha was talking Tommy ear off. Katie just sat there until it was time for the movie to start. We got out the car and went to stand in line to buy the tickets. Tommy had porcsha on one arm and Annie on the other. So why we were in line some guys asked Tommy if he needed some help. No I got this. But porscha just had to say something no he don't need no help this is our man. Tommy couldn't stop smiling yeah baby tell them. We paid for our tickets and went to the bathroom and Tommy said cuz I owe you big time. So which one do you want man I don't know? See porscha is fine but Annie is too and she is thick I don't know what I'm going to do. You are going to have to make your mind up before long. I could have both of them. Now you know that's not going too happened so let me know which one you want. We left out the bathroom stop at the food stand and brought some popcorn and pops. The girls came out the bathroom and came over where we were. Tommy had trouble on his hand choosing which girl he wanted because both of these girls were fine. Katie asked me which girl did he liked the most and I told her I didn't know. We went to our seat to enjoy the movie. When we got in to sit down porscha sat on one side and Annie on the other side. About the middle of movie Tommy said he had to go to the bathroom and asked me to go with him. When we got in the bathroom and he said he thinks he wanted porscha so I said cool. Then he turned around and said no I think I want Annie. No man you have to make up your mind you know you making me miss the movie. Ok I made up my mind I want to be with porscha ok you sure. I'm sure we went back to our seats but Katie couldn't wait for me to sit down I said be cool. Watch the movie what did I miss I'm not telling you until you tell me what he said. He didn't say anything about them he just wanted to smoke. But you think he likes my cousin or do you think he likes porscha. I don't know but when the movie is over we will know. The movie was all most over and Tommy started to make his move on porscha. But she wasn't in to him she told him she had a man. She says that you know my man. What's up cuz she says you know her man. Oh her still mess with Marvin didn't know oh well you better jump on Annie. While you still have a chance. But don't let her know that you tried to come on to porscha. So he tried to come on to Annie she was digging him and beside she's my girl's cousin. Plus she and Katie always hung together so she just kicked it with my cousin keeping it all in the family. The movie was over and when we got in the car Tommy told Annie to get in the front. Porscha didn't like that at all she said take me home. When we got in front of porscha building she gave Tommy her number. Call me Tommy said ok. I don't know who she think I am and threw her number right out the window. I made up my mind who I wanted to be with right baby looking at Annie. Damn right baby hey Katie you see the way porscha was acting when he told me to get in the front seat. It was cool with her when she was in the front seat. He came out here to be with me from what I hear right Katie. I don't know who told her to come along anyway. That's Katie's friend don't start Priest. You know that's your buddy too. Yeah I know her and she was my buddy until she thought I wanted Marvin's ass. Hold up when all this shit happen. Two days after you left to move to the city. Why you didn't tell me, because it wasn't a big thing to me see this is what happened we were having a house nation meeting and I got to the meeting first 20 minutes before her ass. So when she came in she asked me what I was doing here. I told her for the meeting how long you been here. I just got here well don't be in Marvin's house when I'm not there. Do you think I want Marvin; well you don't have a man since Priest moved away. That don't mean a thing Priest is still my man and he's in the city. Plus if I wanted a new man it would not be Marvin's ass. So as I was talking Marvin and the rest of the crew comes in the room so we stop talking. When the meeting was over I left and didn't say anything else to her until today. She asked to go to the show just to see if you were really coming out here. Get the fuck out of here I wish you would have told me that before she got out this car. I would have checked her ass. Nobody wants Marvin ass but her dumb ass. Do you want something to eat? Yeah hey Tommy let's go to big boys what's big boys man. Cuz you're in for a big treat they got the best food in town for real. I haven't had big boys in a long time. You're going to love it. Just drive to Lincoln highway and make a right. We pulled up in the parking lot and I had forgotten that this was one of our kicking spots. The lot was full of people Tommy was like dam what is all these people doing here. It's like this every weekend. We got out the car and everybody was like what up Priest we were just talking about you. A lot of my friends were out there I talked to them for a minute then went in to get our food. Tommy and the girls got us a table by the window. They looked out at everybody kicking it in the parking lot. Tommy says man we need to come out here on the weekend to kick it. That cool with me you got the car. The lady brought us our food we sat and eat and just talked as we eat. Then my old crew came in. what's up Priest we thought we weren't going to see you again. You know better than that I got to come out here to see my people. Plus my girl live out here I got to come and see her about 2 times a week. I got to keep my baby happy. Yeah man it not the same without you being here. I'm just a phone call away. Then we finished our food and left to drop the girls off. On the way dropping off Annie she told us that her mom would be gone for the whole weekend next weekend and we could come and kick it. Everybody said cool Tommie was glad that the girls didn't live far from each other we made it to Annie house he got him a kiss before she got out the car. Katie lives just over the hill from Annie. So we drop Katie off and hit the highway. On the way to the city we kicked all the way home. We talked about what we were going to do with the girls next weekend and before we knew it we was at home. It was a little after 10 when we made it home. You can tell it was late because the kids were in the house. Tommy asked me if I wanted to go with him to make some more money at Michael. No man that was my one and only time selling drugs. I didn't like people who sold drugs because before they sold drugs they didn't have a pot to piss in and when they start to get money selling drugs you can't tell them shit. They live mostly in the east heights you see them all the time at the bowling alley. Wearing the troop jackets and driving their slick cars. They use to think they were better than us because all we use to do is throw parties to make money. They sold drugs to get their money. They use to come to all the parties. they worked for this guy name Otis Moe. I liked him he was cool but his workers I couldn't stand his guys though. What I really liked about him was he didn't act like he was better than us. He would get him a female from the party and leave. Otis knew my brother mike I meet him one day he came to a party with Markey, and I was on the wheels of steel and he gave me fifty dollars to play this song he liked I thought that was cool. He became my nigga after that. Mike use to drive his Corvette sometimes, and when he did he would come and get me and we would ride around and kick until he had to take it back. I knew one day he would put Mike on so he could make some money, but I left before I could see that happen. Being in city was much better for me because I was around my family, and I didn't have to hear a lot of the bullshit that I had to listen to out there. I told Tommy I was going in the house and he told me to tell my auntie that he was going over Mike house, and that he'll be back in the morning. I went in the house and everybody was sleep except Auntie Ruth and her husband Deck. I gave Auntie Ruth a kiss on the cheek and told her I was going to bed. She said good night and then I turned around and went into the room. When I lay down, I heard a hard knock at the door, it was Mona'. She yells through the door, "come on Momma, the police got Mike and Tommy". So we put on our clothes and went over to Mike's house. When we got there we saw police everywhere. They hadn't brought them out of the building yet, but we were waiting when they came out. They had Mike and they even had Brenda Sanders in handcuffs, but no Tommy in sight. I looked up the block and there was Tommy waving his hand in motions for me to come to him. I ran to where he was, and he told me what happened. He said he had seen the police when they ran into the building and that he told mike to run, but he couldn't because he didn't have his clothes on, so he left Mike, he ran down the back stairs but heard the police coming up the back so he acted as if he was leaving out of an apartment on the second floor and they passed him by, then he ran up to the next block. After he finished telling me what happened he then gave me his keys and asked me to go get his car because he wasn't sure if the police was looking for him or not. So I did as he asked me to and went and got the car. I met him on the next block and we drove home. On the way home Tommy told me that could've been him getting into the back of the police car. He then made a joke and said, "man I know you glad you didn't come too", I replied, "hell yeah man, I can't be going to jail and just got here. I don't want aunt Ruth looking at me saying I can't be having this, coming up to police stations getting you out , I don't need then type of problems. Man I can hear her now". We laughed and he said, man you right she'll snap on you. It didn't take long for us to get home and it was late so we went in the house. Auntie Ruth and uncle Deck came in about a half hour after us. They had Brenda with them and she was crying about Michael, they hadn't even noticed we were in the house. We parked the car on the other side of the house. I walked out of the room and Aunt Ruth was like how you get in the house, so I told her Tommy let me in. She then asked was Tommy in there, so I said yes mama. So as I turned to walk away she told me to tell him to come here so I went and woke him up. He walked in the front and Aunt Ruth was filled with joy she said that she had thought the police had him somewhere beating him up. He told her the same story he had told me, she laughed so hard and looked at me and said that why you didn't go over there with him yes mama, you do have a little sense. Cause if you got caught up there with Michael you would be sitting right beside him. I'm not going to get Michael and I wouldn't came and got you either. Let those nigga's he was selling drugs with go get him out. I got some money and I'm going to get him out Brenda said. Aunt Ruth looked at her like she was crazy. I'm going to bed now. The next morning when I got up Tommy was already gone to work. Besides aunt Ruth wanted me to go shopping with her. We rode up north to a second hand store. She was going to get some stuff for the church like glasses and some other things they needed. I loved Aunt Ruth she had a good heart and besides she was my pastor and she was a real pastor. We talked all the way home about me not going over to Michael's and that made me feel good. We stopped at the store to play her lotto. When we was going in the building. suzette was coming down the stairs. Priest you coming over later to listen to some music yeah I'll be over. When she left out the building Aunt Ruth asked me if I liked her yea that's good she's a good woman. I know she's real respectful lady. I took the stuff we bought in the house and left to go on the front it wasn't anyone in front of the building but me. This girl name Betty was coming up the street. What you doing sitting out here by yourself I don't have anything else to do. I'm going to put my books up and I'll be right back. She must have thrown her books on the floor by the front door because she was right back. We sat and talked a long time. Then I was getting the feeling that she liked on me. So I asked her yeah like a brother. That's cool because you like Tommy anyway. Who told you that he did. he knows I like him why haven't he tried to talk to me then. He thinks I'm too black. I don't know ask him when he get off work I will. After she said that Tommy comes driving up in front of the building. What's up cuz hey Betty what you guys up to. What you guys doing sitting out here by yourselves. I was already out here when Betty came looking for you. Get out of here Priest you know you like him Betty. Tommy you know Betty likes you o why don't ya'll stop playing and tell each other how ya'll feel. I'm going upstairs to get me some water so you two can talk. While I was upstairs I call Katie to see if she made it home from school. Nobody answered so I knew she didn't make it home yet. When I got back down stairs they were talking. That's all ya'll have to do in the first place. Tommy asked me if I wanted to ride with him but I thought about it I didn't want to leave Betty out there by herself. I told him to wait until Betty's cousin comes. I don't want to leave her out here by herself. Alright I got to go change clothes anyway and went upstairs. Betty hit me and said why you told him that I liked him. Because if I didn't you would have not did it. I think if my cousin had to be with a girl I think it should been you I think you are a nice girl. We talked a little bit more and Betty's cousin came. Tommy comes back from changing his clothes and we got in the car and drove around the hood. Next weekend I think I'm going to take Betty to church with me. We started back to the house it was time for dinner. We got to the house and went to wash up for dinner. It was time to eat about the same time the lottery came on. The next thing we knew aunt Ruth started jumping up saying thank you Jesus thank you Jesus she had hit the lottery. She had won a lot of money I didn't know how much but it was enough to buy a house in Bellwood. She payed off the deed to the church and gave us all some money. Two weeks later we moved to Bellwood aunt Ruth had even bought her a car. I and Tommy would still come hang out around the old hood. One day not long after aunt ruts tell me have I needed to get a job? And stop sitting around doing nothing I couldn't trip because she was right. So I went and got myself a job it didn't pay well but it was a job. I had gone through a lot of jobs until I found something that I liked. I found a job working as a DJ at a club called the thunder birds. When I wasn't working I use to go in there to party. I met this guy and he hooked me up with the head owner and got me every Friday and Saturday to spin. When I first got the job aunt Ruth didn't like it because she knew it was in a night club but she didn't trip. I was making good money four hundred for the two nights. That was good money for two nights of work. Aunt Ruth put me out of the house after a couple of week of this job guess she couldn't handle it being my pastor in all. I had to end up moving in with Tommy and his girlfriend but I didn't mind because I loved being at the clubs. The thunder bird was the number one club on the Westside. I was only 19 and I didn't drink but This club had the finest females to come in it that I had ever seen. I loved it plus I made good money. I and rick had become real close he understood me. He was the only person that I would sit and talk about my problems. He knew about how my mother and father died and how I was from group home to group home. Rick had told me that he would help me find my brother Curtis he knew everybody on Monroe Street. Everything was going good every time rick went shopping for his self he brought me something. Rather I had money or not. Then one day I and Tommy got into it and he put me out. I didn't have anywhere to stay and rick took me in to live with him and his family. It was good he treated me like I was his son. He made sure I had everything I needed. He had two son named mankey and stuff they were two of the badest kids I had ever seen in my life. They were 5 and 7years old. These little kids use to curse and doing shit I never seen a five or seven year old do. I use to babysit from time to time but I didn't mind. They were cool to have around as lil brother's we would go to the park and people would look at me like I was crazy when they would hear them curse each other out. They would say are those your kids. No they are my little brother's. Why are they cursing each other out? Before you knew it everybody knew them as my lil brother's. I would have to take them to school and pick them up but didn't mind because I would drive Rick's cars. Rick had a nice car's with 30's on them and a nice paint jobs. The sounds were awesome. I would get a lot of girls attention driving the car's all at the bus stop. The minute they found out it wasn't my car I didn't get any more attention. I had made my mind up that I liked living a trouble free life. Making good money babysitting making great money on the weekends. Tommy tried to get in good with me. He saw the money I was making but I didn't stay mad with him, but I didn't move back in with him. I was getting to know my new friends and family. I was really digging the thought about meeting my real brother my dad had told me about. Now everybody knew me on Monroe so that's where I spent my free time. I had met these two dude's name Marvin and pat. I liked these two cats they always had something funny to say. They were unknowns too, that's another reason I liked them. They knew my man ken doss when he was alive we use to sit on Monroe and joke all night long straight kicking it. Until somebody from their family would make them come in. Rick use to always come right on time. We had some good times pat use to roast me real hard. It was just like that. One day this girl from off 33rd block name Kim had walked past. She had just moved on the block. We all got up walking down the street with her to the Madison store. Just talking trying to see who could pull her. Marvin was trying to be mister cool. Now that was some funny shit. She looked at my black rayon shirt and said she liked it. Marvin really was a cool daddy trying to outdo me. But too good to be true rick pull up and told me to get in. Right then I knew something was wrong because he was too early. I got in the car and he reached under the seat and pulled out a gun. He handed me the gun and speeded off and said Tasha just got into it with some nigga's. It was raining by now he was going so fast that we spend around about three times. When the car came to a stop I looked at him and said what you trying to kill us. I could tell by the look on his face that spin had him scared. We made it in front of the building it wasn't anybody out there. It was two girls looking out the window and came running out there. Rick did you hear what had happen. Yea and where's Tasha. She's in the house he goes in the building. I stood in the hallway talking to the two girls that came out. Come to find out those girls were rick sisters. That lives in the same building, right upstairs. I told them who I was and they took me upstairs to meet the rest of the family. They told the people who was in the house that I was Rick's God son. I got a chance to meet Rick's mother she was a nice person when they introduced me to her. He had a brother that didn't live with his mom. He stayed on Chicago Ave. in a big six unit building. Rick had about six cars that he would let family drive sure was happy about that. I got to know everybody that had something to do with rick. Rick had this one friend name Southside he was one of the funniest dudes I knew. He had another friend name lil Willie who had a daughter name Lana who was one of the finest women I had ever seen before she was so cool. She was one of the first women who were part of the thunderbirds crew. Most of the people that were with the crew were older people. Like Walter teller who was the president of the club. Most of them cats were in their late 40's. But who really made the club jump was the people in slickass Rick's inc. like Mallet Tasha and so we were the younger ones of the thunderbirds. We all worked for rick I spin on the wheels plus they made lots of money selling something but I didn't know what it was. All I know is that I wanted to be part of it. Rick wouldn't let me be part of that though. He would tell me you don't need to be a part of that you just keep spinning the records and you; I'll be cool with that. So I took his advice and didn't get in the game. So one day we went over to one of Rick's God sister's house. When we got there rick introduced me to her. Hi my name is Jackie she had a real good spirit about herself.

She said to me if you are Rick's God son you can come by anytime. We sat around talking for a while then another girl came over and got in the car with us. She introduced herself to me. My name is Dee Dee Jackie tells her that I was there little brother. Deeded said we don't need no more brothers we need some more nigga's. I'm just playing with you and she laughed. I'm please to meet you. Deeded just didn't know I didn't want to be her lil brother either. I wouldn't mind being her man but I didn't want to step on anybody's toes. So I kept my thoughts to myself we stayed and talked a little bit more. Rick said come on it's time to pick up the kids. We got in the car and I dropped him off at home. I kept on my way to the school on my way I saw Kim. that's the girl me and Marvin was trying to get up with before rick came and got me that day I asked Kim did she want to ride to the school with me. She got in the car when we got to the school. Mankey was already outside he got in the car and he and stuff start to do what they always' do curse each other out. Kim looks and made them stop that cursing. I couldn't believe it they listened to her. I dropped her off at her house and told her I'll be back later. Went home to take the boys but when I got there rick wasn't home. His sister Kim told me that rick said bring them up to the thunderbirds. We rode up there but when we got there it was a lot of car parked outside the club. We get out and go in rick tell me to be quiet I look in the back of the club. It's a lot of people back there rick what's going on. They are having a meeting, what kind of meeting. A vice lord I just looked I knew a lot of the brothers from off Monroe. Some of the guys asked me why weren't I back there at the meeting. I don't know well be at the next one on next Friday. I said cool the meeting was over and they all left. Rick asked was I a vice lord I told him yea what kind he asks. Unknown then he laughed and said well be your ass at the next one. Wouldn't miss it for the world and we both laugh. I couldn't wait till next Friday. I went and sat up for the party we were having later. Everybody had left and it was the thunderbirds mc's left in the club so I put a tape in so I could make a mix tape and Started making a mix tape for the party it was always good to have one. Didn't know when you might have to go to the bathroom or leave the booth for a minute. I had finished one side of the tape when I noticed everybody was gone out the club next thing I know it was a lot of people in the club I didn't know. But I didn't pay any mind people always come in. and out the club house finishing up the other side of the tape when I look up there is old school spider. He was the chief lil brother from the unknowns. I thought he should have been chief he uses to put me up on what was going on in the nation back in the day. I met spider when I was a little guy he use to live in my aunt's building he use to date this lady name Rose. Rose had got killed and everybody thought he did it but me. I use to be at their house all the time and I knew he loved her. I thought that someone was trying to get spider and they got her and every since I was his lil guy. Nobody would talk to him but me and he loved me for that. I see you are still into records when I and rose use to let you come to our house to listen to music. I've wouldn't never thought you would be a DJ. You sure do sound good too. What's up with you spider how you doing. I'm alright man Priest you sure have grown up last time I seen you. You were a lil guy now you tallest as me. What brings you up here? I'm up here with my brother he came up here to talk to rick. Oh he's my godfather. Oh yea. Do you want to meet my brother yea wait let me finish this tape I'm making for the party. It'll only take a minute. We walk up to the front of the club to where his brother was. I had never seen him before. I just had heard about him, but when I seen him face to face I knew right away who he was because he looked just like spider. And I laughed he say what's funny lil brother. I can't help it but you and spider looks just alike. Are ya'll twins, no just brothers so you the DJ around here. Yes sir, I like that you got respect for your elders. What's your name priest sir oh I got a good friend name priest you know him. What you doing around all these motorcycle people. Rick is my Godfather. All yes that's cool rick my man. Is that who taught you how to DJ. No I learned in school he just gave me a job here. Okay I'll be back later and have this place jumping. Yes sir they left and I finished making my tape. Rick came over to the DJ booth and told me to come with him. We went back to the house and went to his room. Close the door he went under the bed and pulled out a big bag and emptied the bag on the bed. It was nothing but money in the bag more money than I ever seen. He counted out ten thousand dollars he put it in another bag. Then we left got in the car and drove to a street right off Chicago Ave. we got there and went into this building. Knocked on the door and a lady came to the door. Come in she was a dark skinned lady. She tell rick not to worry he needed the money for his lawyer. But I didn't know what she was talking about and I didn't ask any questions. Because it wasn't my place too. She asked me would I like something to eat. No thanks would you like some cookies yea go in the kitchen and get you some. When I went into the kitchen I could hear them still talking. I came back in the front where they were and sat down. Somebody knocked on the door she answered the door. It was a young guy he was about the same age as me. But while I was in the kitchen I could hear her ask rick could he trust me. He told her yes that I was his god son. The dude that knocked on the door came in and went to the back of the house. Didn't know what he was doing either just sat or watched everything that was going on. Then it was another knock on the door she said who is it he said von. She opened the door it was a dude that I had seen before but didn't know his name. Until he came in and gave rick a hug. He went into the kitchen and made him a plate and came and sat back with us. Von's mother was in the room with us too she told me and von to go upstairs so they could talk grown folks talk. We got up and went upstairs. Von turned on the TV we were watching TV and talking. He asks where I was from and was I an unknown vice lord. I told him yea is there a lots of girls where you hang out. But anyway von's mother sent for me because rick was ready for me. I went back downstairs and it was a lot of people down there. Spider was one of them he said man you be everywhere. Von said you know my uncle spider do he know me that's my lil nigga. I just smiled and left out the door. We went and got in the car rick said go upstairs and tell the lady that I was talking to, to come to the car. I went and got her when she got to the car Rick handed her the bag with the money in it and told her to give it to Willie. She put it under her clothes and gave him a kiss. We then pulled off. about a block away we see a police sitting in his car by himself. Rick say is that cronie. I didn't know what the hell a cronie was. He turned off that block and got on the phone to call back to the house we just left to tell them to be careful. Because cronie was sitting on the block. We went back to the club so I went back to the DJ booth to finish my mix tape. So I asked Rick could I use the car to go back to the house to change clothes. You know I didn't go straight to the house. Rode around to listen to my mix tape that I made on Rick's booming tape player. I drove and hit a couple of blocks and ran up on Kim. Hey where you going after you finish here. Oh back to the club, can I ride with you? Yes. I changed clothes. When I got to the apartment Tasha started cursing me out. She thought I was rick. Priest where in the hell rick ass is at. He's at the club she got on the phone and called him. Tasha was Rick's wife While I was in the bathroom washing up I hear her going off on rick about me using his car. I couldn't understand why she was fussing at him about me using his car when she had her own car. Tasha knocked on the bathroom door I open it. She handed me the phone rick say give Tasha the keys how I'm I going to get back to the club, give her the phone. I handed Tasha the phone back. I hear her say I don't know I'm not giving him my keys. Then she says I'll drop him off. When I get out of the shower her and Rick was still on the phone going at it. She hand me the phone and her car keys and say don't fuck up my car. Rick is on the phone saying Priest priest did she give you the keys. I put the phone to my ear and said yea. Good get your ass down here. People have started to come in already. So I leave stop and get Kim. Hey can Mallet come to yea let's go. On the way I see Tasha, hey Tasha I need that mix tape out of there. Let me listen to it, I need it for the club tonight but it's one at home in the stereo in the living room. Cool and we drove off when we got to the club Rick was spinning hey you want me to take over. No so I went to get me a pop from the bar. Hey Priest you want a beer Kim asked. No thanks I don't drink but you can buy me pop. Went got on the dance floor but here comes Jackie and her dance crew. They got on their custom made t—shirts with their crew names on the front and name's on the back. Hi priest and I looked rick was calling me to come and take over the DJ booth. So the first thing I do is give a shout out for the low down crew. Next thing I knew everybody wanted their crew to have a shout out and by all their names. So I did my thing on the booth that night feeling real good about how things were going. Had a place to stay and I loved staying with Rick and his family? I had made a name for myself in the nation and everything. Was good then that one day came Rick asked me to ride to court with him. We talked on the way and we were sure that he was going to beat the case. But when the judge talked she found him guilty. My heart almost broke right in two. I didn't know what I was going to do. Then I thought to ask the guard could I talk to him before he took him up. He did I'm crying by now hey man what you want me to do. Take my keys and get yourself home give Jackie my car keys look out for my kids. I rode all the way home thinking and crying. When I get to the building Jackie and deeded was on the porch. They notice me crying and come over to the car. I tell them what had happened. Next thing I knew it was crowed out there and just about everybody out there were crying. A guy walks up I've seen him around the club sometimes. Jackie talked to him and told him who I was. He walks over to me and tells me who he was and asked me about what happened. We start to walk away from the crowd. I tell him why Rick didn't want Tasha with his car and that I didn't have to move out. Dude drove a nice gold delta 88. We sat there waiting on rick to call everybody that worked for rick was out there. Thunderbirds mc's the delta boys crew everybody. Some of us left to go get something to eat. Everybody couldn't leave because we didn't want to miss Rick's call. Got back with the food and eat the phone rings and it was rick. I was glad he tells Jackie to give me the phone. Hey lil man don't worry I've already told Tasha that you better be there when I get there. Now give Curtis the phone. Curtis is the guy with the gold delta 88. Rick talked to him on the phone, when he got off he take me down stairs and talk to me and tell me to give him the car keys. He told me that blow was going to talk to me. Blow was a fat man Rick's right hand man. I knew he was going to be taking over Rick's business while Rick was locked up. The judge had given Rick three years. He had told Curtis and blow to look out for me already before they had locked him up. So blow finally talks to me and then me him and Curtis goes out to dinner so we can talk. Curtis gives me his car keys and tells me how to put the alarm on and not to worry. And blow was going to take real good care of me until my godfather comes home. I thanked them and they took me home. When I got to the house I thought Tasha was going to act crazy. But to my surprise it was like she was a different person. She had me dinner put up. I said thanks then she went to bed. Watched TV for a while just thinking I fell asleep. The next morning when I got up to take the kids to school. Tasha had already got them dressed and she said I'll take them today but I'm going to leave the top lock unlocked. Priest makes sure you lock up good when you leave. I felt sorry for Tasha Rick was her back bone and she was already missing him, me too. Sat around the house awhile then decide to call and see how my girlfriend Kim was doing. I Was on the phone with her when the other Kim knocked on the door Rick's sister I told her I was on the phone talking to my girlfriend Kim on the phone. She laugh and say with a name like that she better be cute because she'll make the rest of the Kim's look bad. My girlfriends hear her and say have her to know that I look dam good get it right. So I ask Kim do she want me to pick her up and she said yea. I told my god sister to stay until I got back. When we got back we go in and they look at each other and say you look alright and laugh. We watch some movies. Then here comes Tasha back to her old self. soon as she comes in the door fussing company you going to have to go. I couldn't trip because I didn't ask. I took my girl friend home told the other Kim that I would be right back. Soon as we get in the car she starts to go off I don't like that bitch. She didn't have to do that. You need to get your own crib. I drop her off at home and go back to the house. Kim and Tasha were still in the house. Tasha still talking shit boy let me know when you going to have company. You know I can't stay mad with your dumb ass. So I still see you Kim. What the hell you talking about I don't care if Rick's ass is in jail I can come down here anytime I want to. Tasha says I can't get rid of this bitch and they both laugh. Kim we sat around watched TV for a while then Kim said she was sleepy went upstairs. Tasha went in her room and went to sleep I fell asleep on the couch. The next five months went by quickly by now we knew what to do Monday thru Friday weekends was open to go see rick and when would get home I would kick it with my girl. A year had gone by and Tasha was back to normal, she had started locking me out the house and treating me like shit. I need to make me some more money, blow wasn't treating me like rick did, and he told me if I needed more money I had to do what everybody else did. That was to sell drugs. I didn't know that way of life because rick kept me away from it. But rick wasn't here now and I needed money, I had to do what I had to do to survive. So I got down selling, when I started I was scared as hell, then I got to know the ropes. It became my second nature; I didn't know selling would be something I like because I used to always hate on it. Because the people around me made me feel that way, because the way they acted when they started making money. The people that I was down wit were real; they didn't act like they were better than other people. We even had some GD's in our camp getting money with us These were just real nigga's doing what they had to do to survive, no like the clowns I used to hang around with, trying to be like the nigga's in the city. Who's parents had money. and Good job's We had to get a job or get on public aid or hustle to get money my girl was knocked up had to find me some where to stay before I be homeless. So I had to do what I had to do. I went from working the street to passing out work to working the tables. People were wandering how I did it, maybe because I never had short money or anything and I was true to me. I didn't have a lot of nigga's riding around with me and the police was on to me. Plus I still had my DJ job and that's what made the different between me and other people. The game had been good to me and better for me when I started hanging around my old school homies. One of my homies named Kalexie was on this record label and he hooked me up with a lot of DJ's I got a lot of hookups through that too. Everything was running smoothly. My boy Donnell had this cousin name Lil Charles that could rap his ass off. So we started up our own rap group called the snypaz. It was me and my homie. We had to go to the recording studio everyday that was a good thing because that kept us out the hood plus we got paid to do it with check stubs. I always kept mine stubs just in case the police would stop me. If I had a lot of money on me they couldn't say it was drug money and take it from me. So I had to have my shit in order. Come to find out that the guy Curtis that came to get Rick's car keys was my brother the one my dad told me about His mom welcome me in and the rest of the family too. Plus the nation of people and folk's are having a peace treaty and the Oprah Show. Need for me to be on it to talk about it. Man it feels good being a thunderbird boy.

Coming soon the thunderbird boy's